Kelly Corrigan is, more than anything, a mother. While her kids are at school, she reads and writes and cooks up elaborate projects for herself. Kelly is the creator of CircusofCancer.org, a website that teaches people how to help a friend with cancer. Kelly lives in the San Francisco Bay Area with her husband, Edward Lichty, and their two daughters.

THE MIDDLE PLACE

At thirty-six, Kelly Corrigan had a marriage that worked, two kids and a weekly newspaper column. Yet Kelly still saw herself as the daughter of garrulous charmer George Corrigan. She was living in the Middle Place — comfortably wedged between her adult duties and her parents' care. But Kelly is shoved into coming-of-age when she finds a lump in her breast — and gets the diagnosis no one wants to hear. When George, too, learns he has late-stage cancer, it's Kelly's turn to look after the man who'd always taken care of her — and to finally take the leap and grow up.

KELLY CORRIGAN

THE MIDDLE PLACE

Complete and Unabridged

ULVERSCROFT
Leicester

First published in Great Britain in 2010 by
Ebury Press
An imprint of
Ebury Publishing, London

First Large Print Edition
published 2010
by arrangement with
Ebury Publishing
A Random House Group Company, London

The moral right of the author has been asserted

Some names and identifying details of people
described in this book have been changed to protect
their privacy.

British Library CIP Data

Corrigan, Kelly, *1967* –
  The middle place.
  1. Corrigan, Kelly, *1967* – 2. Breast- -Cancer- -Patients
  - -Biography. 3. Breast- -Cancer- -Patients- -Family
  relationships. 4. Large type books.
  I. Title
  362.1'9699449'0092–dc22

  ISBN 978–1–44480–440–9

Published by
F. A. Thorpe (Publishing)
Anstey, Leicestershire

Set by Words & Graphics Ltd.
Anstey, Leicestershire
Printed and bound in Great Britain by
T. J. International Ltd., Padstow, Cornwall

This book is printed on acid-free paper

Most everything I do these days is
dedicated to Edward and the girls,
but this book is for Phoebe,
who wouldn't let it go.

Prologue

The thing you need to know about me is that I am George Corrigan's daughter, his only daughter. You may have met him, in which case just skip this part. If you haven't, I'll do what I can to describe him, but really, you should try to meet him.

He's Catholic. That's the first thing he'd want you to know about him. Goes to church many times a week. Calls it 'God's House' and talks about it in loyal, familiar terms, the way the Irish talk about their corner pub. It's his local. When he was seventy, he became a eucharistic minister, so he helps Father Rich hand out the host a couple times a week. Sometimes, a parishioner named Lynnie looks at him with a certain peace in her eyes, and when my dad tells me about it, he gets misty.

You also need to know about the lacrosse thing. He's in the Hall of Fame, partly because he was an all-American in 1953 and 1954 but mostly because now, in his retirement, he marches up and down the field of my old high school, Radnor, side by side with a guy thirty years his junior, coaching the kids who want to be lacrosse stars. I've watched a hundred games sitting next to him; both my brothers played for years. Not being an athlete myself, I am amused by how attached he is to the game. He remembers every play and can talk about a single game for hours. The words don't mean much to me, but the emotion needs no translation.

And he's a Corrigan. He was one of six loud, funny kids who broke out of a tiny house on Clearspring Road in working-class Baltimore. All athletes, except Peggy, who was a beauty, and Mary, who was a comic. The others; the four boys, played ice hockey in the winter and lacrosse in the spring. The house had three bedrooms — one for the parents, one for the girls, and one for the boys. There was a single bathroom where they bathed, one kid after another, in an old tub of lukewarm water once, maybe twice, a week. My uncle Gene, who made a career out of college athletics, often jokes that the real appeal of sports were the hot showers and new clothes once a season.

And I guess it helps to know that my dad was a sales guy. He sold ad space in women's magazines for fifty years, before there were sales training programs, Excel spreadsheets, and cell phones. He just settled into the front seat of the Buick with a mug of Sanka in his hand, a map on the passenger seat, and a list of his accounts in his head. He kept a box of fresh magazines in his trunk at all times, always prepared to turn a casual acquaintance into a new account. He'd call in to the office from pay phones along I-95 to tell his secretary, the nearly bionic Jenny Austin, how many pages Noxzema signed up for or ask her to send the Folger's people a mock-up of next month's magazine or see if the guy from Stainmaster Carpets called back yet. People loved him.

Toward the end of his career, he changed jobs and got a new boss, a well-trained MBA who favored e-mail and databases. My dad didn't type. He didn't show up for weekly meetings. He couldn't tell you the address of his buddy at Cover Girl and didn't know exactly how to spell his last name. But some months, he sold a quarter of the ad pages in the issue, so who could complain? Despite his billings, he frustrated this particular boss every day for five years, until finally, at sixty-nine, he retired, writing 'Bye Gang!' in the dust on his computer screen.

So there are a few people out there who don't like George Corrigan. That boss is one. I think another might be Bill, his neighbor. Bill yells at his kids, really berates them. Weekends, holidays, snow days, it doesn't matter. I think my dad finds this unforgivable. Or maybe it's that Bill is unamused by my dad. He may even think my dad is nothing but a joker, what with that huge easy chortle of his that floats over to Bill's backyard in the summer when we're out on the deck having a Bud Light.

But the neighbor and his last boss are really the only two people I can think of offhand who don't like my dad. So for thirty-some years, I have been stopped at the gas station, the farmers' market, the swim club, to hear something like: 'You're George Corrigan's daughter? What a guy. What a wonderful guy.'

I think people like him because his default setting is open delight. He's prepared to be wowed — by your humor, your smarts, your white smile, even your handshake — guaranteed, something you do is going to thrill him. Something is going to make him shake his head afterward, in disbelief, and say to me, 'Lovey, what a guy!' or 'Lovey, isn't she terrific?' People walk away from him feeling like they're on their game, even if they suspect that he put them there.

He does that for me too. He makes me feel smart, funny, and beautiful, which has become the job of the few men who have loved me since. He told me once that I was a great talker. And so I was. I was a conversationalist, along with *creative*, a notion he put in my head when I was in grade school and used to make huge, intricate collages from his old magazines. He defined me first, as parents do. Those early characterizations can become the shimmering self-image we embrace or the limited, stifling perception we rail against for a lifetime. In my case, he sees me as I would like to be seen. In fact, I'm not even sure what's true about me, since I have always chosen to believe his version.

I could have gone either way. As I said, I was not an athlete, and just an average student. I was a party girl who smoked cigarettes, a vain girl who spent long stretches in front of the mirror, cutting my own hair, as necessary, before parties. More than once, I stole lipstick or eye shadow from the pharmacy. I used my mom's Final Net Ultra Hold Hair Mist without permission and to outrageous effect. I was suspended from high school for a week as a sophomore for being drunk at a semiformal. I had fallen down the staircase, baby's breath in my hair, new suntan panty hose ripped up the back. A wreck of white polyester.

My dad came to pick me up. As I recall, he was unruffled. It would've been ludicrous for him to say something like 'I am very disappointed.' He wasn't disappointed, or even surprised. This kind of thing happens every so often with teenagers.

My mother, on the other hand, was truly beside herself. She had grown up in a strict German household, where behavior of this sort would have merited a month, maybe two, in the cellar. She had put in a lot of long hours making sure I was not the kind of girl who'd do something like this. I remember hearing my parents argue the morning after the dance.

'Mary, you can't ground her for a month. She's going to be so embarrassed at school, you won't have to punish her.'

'You *must* be kidding me. Are you telling me you think it is *okay* for our fifteen-year-old daughter to get drunk at a school function?'

'Mary, come on.' He laughed as he said it. 'You think she was the only one there who had a few beers before the dance?'

'Absolutely not. I am sure that ninety percent of those kids had something to drink before the dance but Kelly *fell down the stairs*, George. She didn't have *a few beers*. She was *drunk*.'

So what I heard my dad say is: she's fine, a normal kid. What I heard my mom say is: she's wild and getting wilder.

The truth was that I was wild but on my way to being fine.

About twenty years later, having become fine, I called my parents from the maternity ward and cried through the following: 'Mom, Dad, it's a girl, and Dad, we named her after you. We named her Georgia.'

Three years after that, almost to the day, I called home to tell my parents that I had cancer.

And that's what this whole thing is about. Calling home. Instinctively. Even when all the paperwork — a marriage license, a notarized deed, two birth certificates, and seven years of tax returns — clearly indicates you're an adult, but all the same, there you are, clutching the phone and thanking God that you're still somebody's daughter.

PART ONE

George Orwell once said
     something about how childhood
  necessarily creates a
false map of the world
    but it's the only map we've got
      and no matter how old we are,
   at the first sign of trouble,
     we take off running for those
     fabulous countries.
  It's like that for me.

1

monday,
august 2, 2004

August is a terrible time to be born. I aspire to be the self-actualized person who no longer needs or even wants her birthday to be noticed. I fight the urge to plan something. *It's so self-serving*, I tell myself. But this one — thirty-seven — this one is shaping up to be the most mundane, uninspired birthday to date and I'm not sure I can leave it alone.

To: The Ladies
Re: Lunch
Date: Monday, August 2, 2004

As I'm sure you've committed to memory, my birthday is August 16. Mine and Georgia's and Madonna's and Menachem Begin's. But this year, I just want to celebrate mine. Could I talk you into meeting me for lunch in San Francisco? Maybe somewhere with a deck that serves an icy noontime cocktail? Lemme know if you can sneak out on Sat August 21 and

I'll get back to you with a locale.
Love,
Kel
PS People bearing gifts will be stoned to death.

Oh well, I think, noting that my childish need for birthdayness won again, *I tried*. I hit send and start my routine: pull on yesterday's yoga pants (I don't actually do yoga), pair them with a new green T-shirt from Costco, toast frozen waffle for Claire, smear bagel with cream cheese for Georgia, water down juices for both, strap girls into car seats, drop girls off at preschool, come home to move things (dishes to shelves, cans to recycling, socks to laundry basket, bills to pile, shoes to closet). By 11:30 A.M., after I've lost the whole morning to a couple dozen five-minute tasks, it's time to head out for pickup and begin the afternoon routine, which is as dull and typical as the morning routine, so I'll spare you.

Edward, my husband of four years and the father of these girls, is in Philadelphia for work. He usually bathes the girls; it's his time with them at the end of each day, and based on what I overhear, it generally starts out pleasant, quickly becomes trying, and then, by lights out, circles back around to delightful. The fact that he puts the girls down 'after a long hard day at the office' makes my mother adore him. As she should. He's full-service.

On this particular night, after washing the crumbs of chicken nuggets off their plates and successfully negotiating a trade of ten lima beans for a handful of chocolate chips, I take the girls up to the bathroom. Georgia likes to wash my hair. She likes to be the mommy. She'd like to wash her little sister's hair too, but Claire won't have it. When Edward is away, I often find that I've been talked into the tub so the girls can pour too much shampoo on my bushy brown hair. This night is such a night, except on this night, as I brush past my breast to get some soap out of my eyes, I think I feel something hard, just there, under the skin. I touch it once, pressing it lightly with the open palm of my hand, and then, after a flash of shock passes through me, I force my full attention to bathing the girls.

My girls are good — one chubby, one scrawny, both funny. Claire is a year and a half old, and Georgia will turn three next week. They seem older, but for different reasons. Georgia regularly confounds me with questions like 'Does *wrecked* mean *ruined?*' and 'What means *language?*' Claire is topping out at the hundredth percentile for height, weight, and head size. They love Van Halen and Play-Doh and fighting over old rubber bands and barrettes they won't keep in their hair. I love them madly and hope they will be older sisters to more kids just like them.

As I dry myself off, I know I have to touch it again, just to be sure I'm wrong. But I'm not and so I start moving at a manic pace, directing the girls in that weird, strained way mothers do in movies when they find out a bomb is about to go off in their basement, right below where their children are blithely playing with their Legos.

'Georgia, honey, I need you to get in your pajamas right now and meet me at the top of the stairs. Claire, pick up that nightgown and bring it straight to me. Let's go, sweetheart. Right this minute.'

As I give them their instructions, I dial my ob-gyn at home. Dr. Birenbaum is also my friend Emily, and she lives about ten minutes away. She answers, and I can hear her ten-month-old babbling in the background. Emily is happy to have us come over and give me a quick feel.

It's late, dark outside. On the short ride over, we listen to the *American Idol* CD that Georgia's friend left in our car. The girls are thrilled to be riding around in their pajamas instead of going to bed. I tell them we are having a dance party at Emily's.

'Mommy? Mommy? At Emily's? When we are having the dance party, Claire can't dance on the table because she could fall and be in a cast. Right, Mommy?' Georgia asks. I had recently impressed Georgia with a story about a boy who broke his leg by jumping on a bed. He had a cast on for six weeks. 'Because she will cry and have to go to the hospital and get so many shots. Right, Mommy?'

I had emphasized how unpleasant hospitals are. Then I hear myself say, 'That's right, Peach. Doctors, hospitals, lots of shots.'

Emily gives me an exam on her sofa. We joke about her husband coming home to find me topless on his couch, arms over my head. I say I was hoping he would be there so I could get a two-for-one. Georgia and Claire are terribly charming, asking if Emily will tickle them too and then trying breast exams on each other. It's probably a cyst, Emily assures me. I leave Berkeley twenty minutes later, relieved to have a doctor involved. Emily will line up a mammogram for me in the next couple of days, just to be sure.

I come home, carry the girls to their beds one by one, and wait for Edward to call from his business trip. He works for TiVo, and he's gone to Philly to negotiate a deal with

Comcast. When he calls, he runs through the highlights of his day — the contract's coming along, stuck on one issue, one of the guys is a real prick. We tell each other how tired we are. He mentions a sore throat.

Then, in a carefully controlled tone, I say, 'So, when I was in the bath with the girls, I was, you know, washing myself, and I found a lump.' As I talk, I touch it again and again, like you would a loose tooth or a canker sore, each time, surprised to find it still there. 'It's hard as a rock. It's so *right there*. You won't believe it.'

I tell him everything Emily told me; that it is hard, which is bad, but it is movable, which is good, and that in younger women, lumps tend to be cysts.

'Okay, that's good. And you have no breast cancer in your family, so that's good. And hopefully you can get a mammogram tomorrow or the next day and we can be sure,' he says, in character. He is a man of reason, my husband. He does not buy into worry. 'It's gotta be a cyst,' he adds. We hang up a few minutes later, both projecting optimism.

Alone in my room, though, I feel the onset of alarm. I lay my whole body across it, to muffle the earsplitting sound. To fall asleep, I read a long article from a ten-year-old *National*

Geographic about Hurricane Andrew in Florida. On the cover, there's a dirty, sticky, sunburned Marine holding a newly homeless toddler. The guy who wrote the article says that over the course of ten days the hurricane revealed itself, starting as just a patch of thunderstorms, then becoming a tropical storm, and eventually showing its true colors as the unstoppable hurricane it was. A local TV reporter named Bryan Norcross stayed on the air for twenty-two hours straight, 'talking his listeners through the most horrifying hours of their lives, telling them how to find safe places in houses that were blowing apart.' I don't usually last for more than a couple of pages at night, but tonight, I keep going until I finish. I have to follow the arc from panic to toil to renewal. I have to get to the end, to the part where the devastation gives way to rebirth. I read this one sentence over and over again, until I am ready to turn out the light:

'Seven weeks after the storm, there are signs of recovery. Many trees are flush with new growth. Power has been restored. It will be a splendid place once again.'

2

I grew up on Wooded Lane, just a mile from Villanova University, in the suburbs of Philadelphia. Wooded Lane has about thirty houses on it, and every one of them is exactly the same; if you knew where the bathroom was in the Wilsons' house, you could find it at the Walshes'. Our house, 168 Wooded Lane, is the last house on the street, one of the original four. It has classy brown shingles on the face, but the other three sides are aluminum siding, which made it an affordable choice for my parents' first and only home.

I have two older brothers, GT and Booker. In some ways they're hard to tell apart. They both live for sports and tell a good story and make every party they go to louder and better. They'll eat whatever you put in front of them, neither of them will ever retire, and they cry when they give a toast.

In other ways, it's hard to believe they are related. GT is a born worrier and Booker appears to be sliding through life like it's a giant water park. GT is savvy and ambitious and always busy. He's been to the symphony and owns a tuxedo and knows the difference between a pinot noir and a cabernet. Booker, a Bud man, may well do the same job forever — he's a gym teacher and a high school lacrosse coach — and would never ask for anything more than a few free rounds of golf a year and a winning season for the Flyers.

Anyway, after Booker was born in a last-minute cesarean, the hospital counseled my parents against another baby. But, the lore goes, my dad wanted a girl so much, they snuck me in. I suppose it's possible they could have had another boy, but it never seems like that when my dad tells the story.

My brothers shared a bedroom, but I had my own, a pink gingham wonderland behind a hollow door from Sears that was covered with Wacky Packages stickers like Shot Wheels race cars and Cap'n Crud cereal. Later, I removed them and covered the stubborn bits that wouldn't peel off with James Taylor quotes, which I copied from the album liner onto thick paper, using a calligraphy pen that didn't make my hand-writing look any more like calligraphy than a Sharpie would have. Because I was very deep, I even burned the edges of the paper.

From my desk, you could look out on the backyard, which must have been the reason my dad wanted the house. It was a big, flat rectangle, with a drainage gully marking one end zone and a small garden marking the other. The yard became known as Lambeau Field, after the stadium where the Green Bay Packers play — I think the Connor brothers named it, or maybe it was the Kelly brothers — but anyway, a thousand games of Shirts and Skins were played back there, and I watched many of them from my bedroom. More than once, I came down to the sidelines carrying lemonade and Nilla Wafers (after changing my clothes many times, fixing my hair, and glossing my lips with a touch of Vaseline). On a good day, when the light was right, before college added things to my body that laziness has created a permanent home for, someone might have called me pretty. Most days, I was just considered one of the many fine girls in the neighborhood.

Lambeau Field was also home to my dad's tomatoes, which he grew every summer.

'No photos today, men! No autographs!' he'd call out to the guys on the field as he crossed the end zone with an armful of stakes. (Celebrity Seeking Respite from Fans was one of his favorite roles. I've seen him play it for Japanese tourists on street corners in New York and little old ladies in the supermarket parking lot, startling and confusing every one of them.)

'Need a hand, Coach Corrigan?' the boys would say, referring to my dad's prized role as head coach of the local youth ice hockey team.

'No, thanks, men. Play on!' My dad would never interrupt a game.

They'd go back to playing, and he'd start positioning his plants and I'd keep tabs on it all, while working on one of my many projects, like making a new *K*E*L*L*Y* sign for my door, or cutting the collar off another T-shirt at just the right *Flashdance* angle.

'Aw shit,' I heard my dad say one day, creating a pause in the game.

'What happened?' Booker asked. And then I heard six guys cracking up.

'Hey! Up here! What happened?' I called down from behind my screen window.

'Dad's tooth flew out!' Booker called back. 'He sneezed out his front tooth!'

By the time I got outside, all the guys were poking around in the dirt, looking for the tooth, and my dad was explaining that his dentist/friend, Punchy Peterson (or was it Ironhead Keating? there were so many nicknames), warned him that if he didn't get a partial plate, one of these days something like this was bound to happen.

'I'm just glad it happened out here with you knuckle-heads and not at a business meeting. Can you imagine old Greenie shooting a tooth across the desk at a customer?' He often referred to himself as Greenie, or the Green Man, which is a nickname his brothers gave him way back after a long, crammed car ride when a case of bad gas reputedly turned the air around my dad green.

The neighborhood guys were kicking around in the garden, laughing through a relaxed search. I was leaning into my dad, who had his arm around me.

'Keep going, men! There's a dollar in it.' At the time, a one-dollar reward could have bought three or four Cokes.

Some guys dug around the dirt, some fingered the grass. I just stood with my dad, since I could get a dollar off him anytime, for nothing. Minutes passed. Commitment waned.

'Men! Let's take it up to two dollars! Two dollars right now for whoever finds the tooth!'

'Coach, what kind of teeth do you have, anyway? I mean, how did it just shoot out of your mouth?'

'Oh God, Timbo. You can't believe the way they used to do things — I mean, I think I had about twenty cavities by the time I was ten years old, and braces for — God — I'm guessing seven years. The guy's office was over a garage. He probably didn't even have a degree — ' he explained, sort of. 'Men,' he called out to the guys who were still in the hunt. 'Let's go for five! Five dollars for that tooth!'

That stepped up the action for a while, but after ten minutes, the hunt was declared hopeless.

'I guess I better call that guy and see if I can get in there today. Carry on, men! Lovey, ride over with me. He'll take better care of me if he sees you,' he said.

When we got to the dentist's office, my dad made a big deal out of introducing me to the secretary, whom he himself had just met.

'Candy, this is my daughter, Kelly Corrigan,' he said, like I was someone Candy would want to know, someone she would remember meeting.

'Hi, Kelly,' she said, playing along.

'Hi.'

'Well, Mr. Corrigan — '

'George! Please, Candy, call me George!'

'Well, if you wait here, George, I think we can get you in, but it might be an hour or so.'

'Tell you what, Candy!' he said, like he was about to announce something exciting. 'Why don't Kelly and I go run some errands and we'll be back here in forty-five minutes?'

'Are you sure?' she said, looking at his six-year-old smile.

'Yeah,' he said. 'Who's looking at an old Billy Goat like me?' When he wasn't referring to himself as Greenie, or The Green Man, my dad referred to himself as 'an old Billy Goat.'

Candy and I made eye contact, and I think I was able to convey to her that although most adults wouldn't bomb around town with a missing front tooth, it was well within the general operating procedures for George Corrigan. Off we went.

After a swing by the Coastal gas station, where my dad hollered a compliment to Pete, the proprietor, about the new flower boxes by the front door, we headed to the farmers' market. The first person we ran into was Frank Tolbert, who was in line at the deli.

'Lefty Tolbert! How you doing?' my dad said, laughing and chomping down on his lower lip like a beaver.

'Good God, George! What happened?'

'Lefty, you wouldn't believe it if I told you! But it's nothing that's gonna stop me next week on the court, so you better work out that kink in your backhand!' Then he turned his attention to the high school girl behind the counter and said, 'You should see this guy try to return my serve. How's the roast beef today? I love that roast beef you guys have.'

She said the roast beef was good, same as always. She tilted her head and raised her eyebrows impatiently, totally uninterested in the story behind the missing tooth, the fact that Lefty had trouble protecting the alley, or that my dad favored this deli's roast beef over all others.

'Um, there's a line,' she said.

'Aw, God, sorry! You're a hardworking gal!' my dad said. 'I'll have one pound of your best roast beef!'

Such was my dad's relationship with the world that he paid more attention to the good stuff than the bad and effortlessly forgave almost all — the peevish girl at the deli, the kids destroying his lawn with their cleats, the daughter who cut her brand-new shirts to look like a Juilliard student.

★   ★   ★

When I was a high school freshman, GT was a senior and Booker was a junior. That year, my dad took over the morning routine from my mom, whose reign involved the usual nagging — time to get up, your breakfast is on the table, don't forget your biology book, I said time to get up, you're not wearing those jeans to school, is that mascara I see on your eyelashes?

With my dad in charge, things changed.

'Lovey,' he'd call out as he pulled the

plastic shades and flipped on the light. 'Let's get to it! It's gonna be a great day!'

If I waited for a moment, he'd be gone, doing the same drill next door with GT and Booker. He'd personalized his appeal with little add-ons like, 'Booker, The Book Man, Citizen Book! Today's the day you're gonna ace that math test!' or 'G, big game tonight! I'm seeing a hat trick!'

When his usual ruckus failed to get feet to floor, he'd walk down the hall to his bedroom and throw open the window. Cupping his hands around his mouth, he'd call out:

'HELLO, WORLD!'

And then, playing back to himself in his one-man show, he'd flip to the role of World: 'Hello, Georgie!'

'I'M COMIN' OUT THERE TO GET YOU, WORLD!'

To which World would respond, as of course World would, 'I'm waitin' for ya, Georgie!'

And then he'd turn around and head back toward our bedrooms, making a certain kind of merry battle cry.

After a couple years of this, I could only deduce that the world was a safe place. In fact, according to my dad, the world was beyond safe — it had a sense of humor, it knew your name, it was waiting for you. Hell, it was even rooting for you.

3

wednesday,
august 4

I wake up with Georgia just inches from my nose, urgently notifying me that Claire is ready to get up. I always love them best first thing in the morning, having forgotten something critical about them in the night, something gorgeous and utterly lovable.

'Claire is crying,' Georgia says.

'Yup,' I say, rolling out of bed. 'That's what babies do. That's how they get our attention.' Together, Georgia and I walk back toward the tiny blue room where Claire sleeps. 'You used to cry all the time. But now you can talk,' I say, selling her on the idea that big girls use words. When we open Claire's door, her face is wet and red with the drama of separation. There are three or four binkies on the floor around her crib. 'It's okay, Clairey. I'm right here. Here we go. Up, up.' I squeeze her so she knows she's safe and then lay her on the bed to change her bloated diaper. 'That's my girl. Are you ready for the day?'

Claire seems ready enough.

After an abbreviated morning shuffle, I hand them off to Sophie, our regular sitter, and make my way to the Alta Bates Imaging Center.

The waiting room is like the DMV with carpet. 'Inspirational' posters are framed in purple along the walls. About twenty women — some bored, some restless — wait to hear their names called. A chipper technician says my name and then explains that she'll be taking two pictures of each breast and it shouldn't take more than a couple of minutes. As she wedges my breast between two metal plates, I say, 'Ever since breast-feeding, my boobs are just empty bags. I bet you can get those plates to kiss.' She seems genuinely impressed as she cranks the plates closer and closer, until they're only four centimeters apart. I'm a C cup, so four centimeters should be making you wince.

She leaves me in there with an *Elle Décor* while she takes my films to the doctor. In the time it takes to flip through the magazine, she's back.

'The doctor asked me to take a few more pictures, so come on up here and let's get it over with — real quick,' she says. I'm suddenly as alert as I would be if I heard my front door open in the middle of the night.

I keep a close eye on her as she

manipulates my breasts. We're just a few inches apart, and it seems reasonable that if she knows something dreadful already, I'll be able to see it, or smell it. I don't ask any questions, like *Is it unusual that the doctor wants more pictures?* or *Was the machine acting up?* But if she looked at me, she could read my face like a breaking-news banner on MSNBC. If she looked at me, she'd know to say something reassuring. She doesn't. She sticks to procedure, and in no time, I am alone again with *Elle Décor*, noticing the weight of the pages and how slick they are. There's an ad for a fancy stainless steel range, with a shapely housewife smiling serenely while sweeping a spotless floor. Her breasts are perfect.

'Ms. Corrigan, Dr. White would like to talk to you about your films. Why don't you put your clothes on and I'll walk you back to his office.' I can practically taste the adrenaline in my mouth as I reach for my bra.

Dr. White — sorry, old, uncomfortable Dr. White — stares at my file while he explains that I should have a biopsy as soon as possible. Behind him, eight-by-ten films of my breasts are tucked into a light box on the wall. I am grinding my teeth.

'I am very concerned about the — well, the *mass*,' he says, pointing to a profile of my breast and specifically to a white, stringy area behind my nipple that looks like a comet with tails. So I must have felt only the tip. 'I am putting you down for a core needle Friday morning, so you will come back to this building then.'

I'd like to know what a 'core needle' is, but I'm more interested in why he's 'concerned.' He says the mass is quite large, perhaps seven centimeters, and looks like an *explosion*. That's the very word he chooses. I feel like a four-year-old who has just spun around in the grocery store and realized that the woman she thought was her mother is a stranger and every aisle she looks down is empty and every voice she hears is the wrong one. Red hot tears start streaming down my cheeks. I can see that my reaction is making Dr. White uneasy but not so uneasy that he offers up any hope. He doesn't say 'Oh, I see I have alarmed you . . . ' He doesn't say 'Don't get ahead of yourself.' He doesn't say 'Many times, these mammogram films are misleading.'

He says, 'You can be here Friday then? At ten A.M.?' I nod, wiping my cheeks with my fingers.

He sends me out to the waiting area while they confirm the biopsy schedule. Sitting there, 'explosion' ringing in my ear, I long for

Monday morning, when my great project was pulling together a birthday lunch, when everything was just as mundane and unremarkable as it could be. The tears just keep coming. I can feel people looking at me, like the lady sitting two seats down. She is thin and tidy and surprised when I tell her I am alone, that I'll be driving a car in a minute, headed home to relieve the babysitter, cook some mac and cheese for the girls. She offers to take me home or call a cab, but I move away from her, unable to stand the kindness.

I can't get out of the room fast enough. I am charged, like a cow in the field that can feel stray electricity coming up through the ground. Tingle voltage, they call it. It happens in pastures where too many electrical wires have been buried, and sometimes the shocks are enough to electrocute the animals. Safe in my parked car, I call Edward.

'Edward, they want me to have a biopsy. On Friday. The doctor said he was 'very concerned.' He said it looks like 'an explosion.' It's like seven centimeters. Seven centimeters, Edward. You know that woman at work? Who had breast cancer? Hers was one centimeter. It was like a — pearl — a pea. Seven centimeters is as long as a credit card, or' — I look at my hand — 'a pinky. He said it had *tentacles*. I saw it — it looked like a piece of fried calamari. He couldn't even look at me, Edward. He never made eye contact.'

Edward has taken my call in the middle of a business meeting; he stepped out of the conference room 'for a minute,' without explanation, and they're waiting for him to return, to press on. For all they know, I am his secretary calling with a scheduling question. No one thinks I am his wife calling from a parking lot about a 'mass' that has 'exploded' in her chest.

'Okay. Um, okay. Well, I should come home. I'll come home. Let me get the flight changed and I'll call you back. Okay?'

The fear is physical — the slight pressure in my eyes, the inability to focus, the shallow breathing. If I were a porcupine, my needles would be so extended I'd be trapped in the front seat.

When I get home, the babysitter is eager to tell me about the morning. I can hear the girls upstairs. 'Okay, like, Georgia, is so smart. She remembers, like, every story I have ever told her — '

I am trying to smile, trying to hear Sophie, look at her, but I am shaky, so I lower my head and push things around in my purse, looking for my wallet, I guess, buying some time, deciding how to ask her about Friday morning.

'So, could you be here on Friday morning?' I blurt out, ignoring her report about Georgia's remarkable recall.

'Yeah,' she says, dropping the story. 'Of course.'

There is a moment of silence. Sophie looks me right in the eye, and I break.

'I have a lump, there's something in my breast, I had a mammogram. They want to do a biopsy. I don't know.'

She hugs me. My seventeen-year-old babysitter is hugging me and rubbing my back. And I am letting her.

★　★　★

Edward is home the next morning. That night, after the girls floor us with the usual routine of relentless questions and tireless squabbling, we work our way toward bed.

'So, how do you feel about all this?' I ask as I pull on my pajama bottoms.

'About the biopsy? I think it'll be fine,' he says, tossing his T-shirt on the floor, about twelve inches away from the laundry basket.

'That's good. I guess.' I don't like his answer. It makes me feel lonely and kind of crazy. I wait for him to ask me how I feel.

'What time is it again, ten A.M.?' he asks.

'Yeah, but we have to leave at nine A.M. so

we can go get the mammogram films beforehand.' I go along with the logistics chatter, but I'm still waiting to talk about bigger things. 'So you just feel super optimistic, like this is a fire drill . . . ?'

'No.' He's on the defensive. 'I just think there is no point in getting too worked up about it before we know anything.'

'I feel worked up about it,' I admit, now also on the defensive. 'I guess you didn't see what I saw yesterday. The mammogram films were one thing, but the doctor, I mean, I told you, he was just so serious. He was *grave*, Edward.'

'Yeah, but, as you always say, Kelly, you don't know what happened in his life five minutes before you walked into his office. He could have gotten in a fight with his boss, or found out his kid got kicked out of college. Maybe his wife just asked for a divorce — I don't know. We just shouldn't overinterpret his mood.' He tosses the decorative sham on the floor and pulls back the comforter.

'Yeah, well, one thing that happened five minutes before I walked into his office was that he saw four pictures of a mass, and he knows, after thirty-five years of looking at these things' — my voice cracks — 'he knows it's cancer.'

'Maybe not, Kelly, maybe *not*. Let's not get

ahead of it,' he says. He settles into reading position, as he does every night. After a pause, where he stares at me to see if I have more to say, he leans over to his bedside table and picks up the new *Sports Illustrated*. The NFL preview issue.

I turn out my light and go silent. The frustration burns. He hasn't picked up a single lead. Or he has, but he just won't take the bait. Or maybe he can't. I start to cry.

I hear the *Sports Illustrated* pages touch the nightstand. 'Are you okay?' he asks. 'Come here, turn around, it'll be okay.' He wraps around me.

I tell him I don't want to turn around or talk about it. 'Why bother?' I don't want to invest the energy in sharing my anxiety, since there isn't any payoff, any recognition, any release. I say this might be one of those things I should just discuss with my girlfriends and not expect so much from him.

He shakes his head and clears his throat. And then he starts. Slowly. The kind of thing you don't interrupt for fear that even lifting your head off the pillow will make the words dissolve back into the shapeless puddle of feeling where they were born.

'Do you want to know what I think about this? Do you really want to know what I thought about on the plane ride home?' He can barely talk. 'I thought about it all, all the way to the end and beyond. I thought if you . . . you died . . . and someday I had to find another wife . . . ' My eyes widen. 'I would be so mad at her because she wouldn't be . . . she wouldn't be you.' We've switched positions. I am wrapped around him now. 'And I thought that no one could touch those girls, no one deserves them . . . no one makes them who they are like you do.'

4

It is one thing to be a man's wife — quite another to be the mother of his children. In fact, once you become a mother, being a wife seems like a game you once played or a self-help book you were overly impressed with as a teenager that on second reading is puffy with common ideas. This was one of many things I had learned since crossing over into the middle place — that sliver of time when childhood and parenthood overlap. One day you're cheering your daughter through a swimming lesson or giving her a pat for crossing the monkey bars or reminding her to say 'please,' and the next, you're bragging to *your* parents about *your* newest trick — a sweet potato recipe, a raise at work, a fix for your ant problem. It's a giant Venn diagram where you are the only member of both sets.

The middle place is also hallmarked by endless, irresistible, often exasperating comparisons between your family of origin and the family you've made. 'My parents would never let us talk to them like that.' 'My mom always insisted that we eat dinner together.' 'My dad spanked us with a wooden spoon all the time and we're fine.' Thanks to these filial imprints, Edward and I have caught ourselves fighting over such minutia as how to cook pasta — set a timer or do a taste test.

By the time I was old enough to bother noticing, my mom and dad had settled into a marriage that was high functioning but not especially romantic. It had all the characteristics of a healthy, established corporation. My mother held the power positions: finance and operations. Her realm covered allowance, dress code, and chores. My dad took care of sales, like convincing us that snurfing (the precurser to snowboarding) down the eight-foot drop into the backyard was as good — better! — than a weekend in Vermont. He also defined our corporate culture. Corrigans, my dad conveyed, were scrappy corner-cutters who could always find a way into any place. They knew how to shake hands and make eye contact and tell a joke. They had reason to be proud. Under his leadership, employee satisfaction was high. My parents' partnership hummed, except on those occasions when Greenie hinted at some elasticity in a standing policy — like, say, curfew — tempting us to push our limit by suggesting that if we were a little late, he'd handle it with Mom.

But that never worked. You'd be there, at

the party, boldly lingering past midnight, maybe even lining up at the keg for one more refill. You'd be ha-ha-ing it and acting like you were a regular kid like all the others, a kid whose parents were home in bed. And then you'd hear his voice.

'Wrap it up, kid. Your mother can't sleep,' he'd say, standing in the door in his Indiana Jones hat and his overcoat, with his oxford cloth pajama pants peeking out the bottom. As you'd put down your beer and poke around for your coat, he'd glad-hand some of the guys and maybe even take a sip of somebody's beer. 'See ya, gang!' he'd say, escorting you out.

As far as taking care of himself, my dad's pattern was general compliance punctuated by brief interludes of opportunism. In other words, if, on a Saturday morning, he mowed the lawn and folded the laundry, then he might decide to play an extra set of tennis or swing by a lacrosse game on the way home. He was always 'swinging by' places. He had a knack for showing up within minutes of my mother looking at the kitchen clock and saying, 'If your father doesn't walk through that door in the next five minutes . . . ' It was uncanny, the way he kept his account balanced. My mom rolled her eyes a lot, but every so often, she would look at him while he was telling a story and smile in such a way that I knew she loved him.

Maybe because they seemed so practical, I often made up stories about my parents' passionate early days, how eager my dad was to have her, how irresistible my mom found his pleas. The facts emerged with the decades. He proposed the night he met her. He had another fiancée. He was unworthy in the eyes of her parents. He vomited on their lawn one night when he was, as they say in Dublin, 'well jarred.' I gathered up those scraps and stitched together a love story that kept me warm enough.

Then, one rainy day when I was a teenager stranded at home without a car, I started rearranging the furniture in my room. This was a fairly regular event, and I had nearly run out of configurations when I noticed an old trunk in GT's room that might look just right at the foot of my bed. It was much too heavy to move, so I began to empty it. There, underneath several heavy wool blankets, were a hundred letters, maybe more. A hundred envelopes to my mother, Mary Dwyer on Newland Road in Baltimore, written in my father's outrageous handwriting. (He prints, usually in all caps, but he never lifts his pen off the page, so every letter is connected to every other letter. Decoding his penmanship is as satisfying as finishing a crossword puzzle.)

I picked up an envelope like you might a feather. The house was silent around me. I had a little buzz, like I had been drinking. The letter was from 1963, when Kennedy was in the White House and Neil Sedaka was fighting for airtime with Frankie Valli.

January 1963

Dear Mary,

It's 30 degrees here. There are piles of snow everywhere. I spent the day slogging it out for the 'big guys' at *TV Guide*. My old friend Ray Tomar at Oldsmobile bought some pages, but all the while, I was thinking of you. I am looking forward to seeing you again at the Burch's luncheon in Philadelphia on Feb 1. Cousin Nancy tells me she will be there. I'm sure she'll drive you down if you want.

Wear that red sweater for the Corri — I love a blonde in red.
Yours,
George

Which brings us to my mother's 'blonde hair,' which we take on faith, since it has been forty years since her hair went untreated. Now, it's more frosted than anything, sort of a snowy color, and always in the same cut, short, lifted off her forehead in a partless roll, sort of like Martha Washington, or, for that matter, George Washington. Anyway, where you might see white, my dad sees blonde, Grace Kelly blonde.

The letters were out of order, so I just opened the next one to touch my fingers. It was from the previous fall, the fall of 1962.

Dear Mary,

You might think that Bob Grady is quite a catch, but I know better! Hopkins guys are stiffs! I can outscore him and outromance him! It'd be a long boring life as Mrs. Grady.

Will you come to the lacrosse game against Mt. Washington next Sunday? I'll put one in the net just for you. My sister Peggy can drive you over.

Truly,
George Corrigan

Bob Grady and my mom? My mom dated other people? My mom was a girl in demand? My mom was a *girl*? I believe these moments are now called paradigm shifts. At the time, I wouldn't have been able to put it into words. *Revolutionary, staggering, gross* — all inadequate.

I kept going, letter after letter, until my mother found me there, surrounded by unfolded pages. It might have been an hour, maybe two.

'Mom, these are incredible! Did you know these were here?'

'Of course I knew they were here, Kelly. They're mine. Now put them away and apologize for snooping,' she said as she left the room, wearing her standard black work pants, the ones from a sale at Macy's six years ago, the ones with the elastic waist. I dug around in the mothballs for one letter that stood out. It had a poem in it. I brought it downstairs. She was at the kitchen table with a glass of Inglenook over crushed ice.

'Okay, Mom, just listen to this one,' I said, atwitter. 'It's a love poem! He wrote you love poems!' I was so gratified to see a real sliver of the romance I'd always imagined. I sat down across from her, and I read it to her against her will, my head down, lost in the verse. When I looked up victoriously at the end, her face was flush with tears.

'Your father — he's something else,' she said, thrilling me by choosing the present tense. Then she stood up, shook her head, wiped her face, and walked to the sink to start dinner.

'I want you to put those back where you found them,' she said as she filled a pot with water. I stared at her for a minute. She had never looked like this to me before, like a woman who would collect all her love letters and pack them away with mothballs so they would last forever.

5

friday,
august 6

It's 4:32 A.M. Five hours and twenty-eight minutes until my biopsy appointment. Edward is asleep next to me. Something about his position makes him look misshapen but I stare at him anyway, happy that he is sleeping, then resenting it. After twenty or thirty minutes, I give up and go to the basement to watch TV. Channel 512: *About a Boy.* Perfect. It's the scene where Hugh Grant crashes the single-parent support group meeting. They are all standing in a circle chanting, 'Single Parents! Alone, Together! Single Parents! Alone, Together!' It's so funny, even though it is slightly misleading. Married people are often alone and together at the same time.

Finally, the morning comes. Edward finds me asleep on the sofa.

'Hey. How long have you been down here?' he asks in a doting way that makes me love him again. 'Do you want me to make you some tea?'

⋆ ⋆ ⋆

I check in with the receptionist while Edward finds us a spot in the waiting room. He unpacks our reading materials, preparing for a wait. As I give my name to the receptionist, I listen to my voice answer each question:

'I'm here for a core needle biopsy . . . '

'Left breast . . . '

'Yes, I have my mammogram films . . . '

'An HMO . . . '

'My husband is the primary . . . '

'Last name Lichty . . . '

'Corrigan . . . '

'Dr. Birenbaum referred me . . . '

From a distance, I watch myself gingerly approach cancer. It is outside me. It is abstract. I fill out the forms, and everything seems so loaded. Who should they call in the event of an emergency? My parents? In Philadelphia?

Edward has only just begun a *Sports Illustrated* article on Shaq and Kobe when they call my name.

'Here,' I respond stupidly, like a kid on the first day of class. I slide my *Real Simple* magazine back into our bag. Just last Saturday, that same tote carried two towels, sunblock, and a swim diaper to the local pool.

For forty minutes, a nervous young doctor

46

jams something that looks like a sixteen-inch harpoon into different parts of my breast while a cheery nurse guides her via sonogram. With a slightly strained voice, the woman with the instrument says things like 'your breasts are so dense, so young, it's hard to get through the tissue.' I am pleased to hear my breasts are dense and young.

A sick part of me actually wants the bad diagnosis, if only to prove that I know my body, that I am not a hypochondriac looking for unwarranted attention. And given the ongoing push-pull with my husband, who sees no danger in the world ('she's not going to crawl out the window') and me, whose imagination runs toward the catastrophic ('we're three floors up!'), I almost want the lump to be a tumor so he sees that sometimes fears are justified. But it's more than that.

I want to know what it would be like. I want to know how I would perform. I remember a Poe story I read in college, 'The Imp of the Perverse,' about this elemental, radical impulse people have. In the story, a man stares into an abyss from the edge of a cliff. At first, he is dizzy with horror. He shrinks back. But eventually, he is consumed with the idea of falling, even jumping, just to feel the rush of the plunge.

Nothing bad has ever happened to me. No

disease, no disorders, not even a broken bone. What would it feel like?

Before we leave, they tell me I'll have significant bruising and show me four tissue worms floating in solution packed up in a little plastic container. The sticker on the lid has my name on it.

On the way home, I close my eyes and pretend to be resting while I secretly take back my perverse thoughts and promise whoever may have heard them that no matter what flashes of curiosity I may have had, I definitely, *definitely*, don't want cancer.

6

The bravest thing I ever did was kill a snake. It was an accident, but it still counts.

The snake came to Wooded Lane the same spring that my dad gathered us around the kitchen table and made this speech:

'So, you all have your chores, yeah?'

'Yeah.'

'And you' — he looked at me — 'want a dollar for every time you take out the trash, right?'

'Right,' I nodded, comfortable with my pricing.

'And you' — he looked at Booker — 'you want ten dollars for cutting the lawn, right?'

'At least,' Booker replied, definitely implying he may have underpriced the project for a good guy like my dad.

'So that's just *passing money around the inside*,' he said, eyebrows raised, slowly nodding, like '*get it?*'

'Huh?' Booker said.

'What?' GT said.

'Dad?' I said.

He stuck to this seemingly self-evident phrasing while he waved his arms around in

49

circles, eyes wide to make his point. 'We're *passing money around the inside.* We're ready to start bringing it in *from the outside.*'

He fished around in a paper bag I hadn't noticed on the counter. Booker slumped over, apparently catching on before I did.

'We're ready to get out there and start drumming up some business on Wooded Lane.' He lifted a grass green T-shirt out of the bag that said CORRIGAN CUTTERS in big white block letters.

'DAD!' Booker whined.

'DAD!' GT echoed.

I stayed quiet. Girls did not cut lawns.

'Corrigan Cutters!' my dad broadcasted, as if it were perfectly obvious. Then he flipped it around to show us the back. THE BEST FOR LESS!

Then he reached back in the bag and pulled out a pink T-shirt that said CORRIGAN CLEANERS . . . THE BEST FOR LESS!

I was appalled. 'Are you *crazy?*'

Fortunately, the cleaning business never took off in the way the lawn business did. I had a couple three-dollars-an-hour gigs up at the Dunlaps', where I wiped down walls while Mrs. Dunlap nursed her third baby from one colossal breast then the other, but that was about it. Booker, on the other hand, saved up fifty dollars in no time and became a

50

man possessed by a dream, a dream to own a boa constrictor.

Booker is the funniest person some people have ever met, people who love John Goodman, *Caddyshack*, and stories about guys passing out and pissing themselves. All this joking around sometimes leads people to assume that Booker is just a laid-back dude who never makes a bit of trouble. For the most part, he is. But when he gets his head wrapped around an idea — I'd say once or twice a decade — he will not back down. The snake thing was the first time I noticed this. Booker was twelve.

He left without fanfare on the R5 train, which took men in suits and women in skirts and panty hose from the Main Line to downtown Philadelphia. Hours later, he appeared in the kitchen, holding a special pet store bag.

'Did you get a hamster?' I asked.

'No, I got a little white mouse' — he paused for dramatic effect — 'and a boa constrictor.'

'Shut up,' I said, breaking a rule that still stands in our family today.

'You shut up.'

'GT!' I wailed. 'GT! GT! Come here right now! GT!' I was moving toward the stairs, away from Booker and his revolting creature.

'What?' GT screamed back at me, throwing open his door and blanketing the upstairs with the sound of Jerry Garcia memorializing Casey Jones, who apparently used to drive a train high on cocaine.

'Scott has a snake!' I used Booker's God-given name.

'No way! Awesome! Fuckin' awesome!' he said as he barreled past me at the foot of the stairs. 'Dude! Book! You did it! You really did it!'

Within an hour, thirteen boys and Kathy Walsh, the neighborhood tomboy, had assembled to witness the first sickening feeding. The snake's body ran the length of an old glass fish tank, maybe twelve inches, and was lazing around on pebbles and sticks from our yard, never moving but breathing visibly. Booker had set him up in his closet, so he could keep a lamp shining on him at all times, manufacturing a comfortable temperature for our new family 'pet.' The audience was three deep, peeking in through shoulders, over heads, under arms. Booker picked up the white mouse kindly, then took its tail and lifted it over the cage, its tiny, clawed feet extending frantically in all directions. The cocky snake barely moved, but when Booker let go, that mouse had about ten seconds of fruitless scrambling before 'Shifty,' as he had quickly come to be known, latched on to the little rodent's hind parts. In a flash, the mouse was fully enveloped, just a silenced lump.

For the rest of my brother's afternoon of fame, I stayed in my room, door double locked, a towel stuffed into the crack. Finally, after I had lost several pounds to dehydration and the raw, electrifying energy of panic, I heard my dad calling for me. They were home.

'Dad!' I called through the door. 'Dad! Come to my door!' He came. I heard him turning the knob without success.

'Lovey?'

'Yeah. Dad, there's a snake in Scott's closet!' My dad laughed. 'Seriously, Dad, there is a snake in Scott's closet! GO LOOK!' I sounded delirious.

'Okay, Lovey, I'll go get it. Just give me a minute to hang up my jacket.' He was walking away. Where were my brothers?

And then I heard it. A door opened and my dad said, more astounded than angry, 'Holy shit! Booker! Where did you get that? . . . Uh — Mary, you better give me a minute up here! Go back in your room, Book. Put it away for now . . . Lovey, everything's okay.'

'MAKE HIM TAKE IT BACK!' I demanded. 'HE HAS TO GET IT OUT OF THE HOUSE!'

My mom was on the stairs.

'Dad, he spent fifty bucks on it.' GT had emerged from his den of hippie music to

53

plead his brother's case. 'It's a foot long.'

'HE TOLD ME IT'S GONNA GROW TO SIX FEET!' I screamed from behind my door. 'SIX FEET!'

A compromise was reached. The snake would be relocated to the back basement, the unfinished half, and a heavy storm-window-cum-tank-cover would replace the flimsy screen Booker had considered sufficient. A small crack was left open for air. It was this small crack that tortured me. My dad let me sleep in his spot, next to my mom, and he took my bed for the night.

I tried to sleep. I tried to stop my imagination from making the movie where Shifty, growing longer and stronger with every mouse, constricted his body, lifting himself vertically along the corner seam of the tank, using his snout to nudge the storm window a little wider so he could slither out and up the stairs to the first floor, and then, finding no flesh there, up the stairs to the second floor, where he would naturally turn left into my parents' bedroom. Smelling me — my horror — Shifty would curl noiselessly up and around the leg of the bed and find an opening in the fold of the bedspread.

I had no choice.

I trembled as I put my feet on the carpet. The fear was nauseating. I strained to see each step as I descended, coming closer and closer to my aggressor. I flipped on the back-basement light, and in a flash, I had moved the storm window an inch or two, completely eliminating Shifty's chance for escape, or oxygen. He never moved, probably sleeping with his eyes open, which is the most foul and conclusive evidence of a snake's wrongness. I hit the light switch again and, closing every door behind me, rushed up the stairs, back into the still warm spot next to my mom. I lay there in the dark, heart thumping, flabbergasted by my own moxie.

★ ★ ★

'DAD! DAD! Come here right now!' Booker screamed from the back basement around 7 A.M. the next morning. 'Dad, Shifty killed himself! He drowned himself! Come look!'

And this is how the story has always been told: Booker bought a defective snake. A depressed snake. A snake not meant for suburban life. On his very first night in his new home, Shifty Corrigan drowned himself in a bottle cap of water.

My mom was on the phone with the pet store manager by 9 A.M., demanding a refund. No one was gonna mess with one of her kids, not on her watch.

7

On Monday morning, a week after I found the lump, Edward asks me when I'm going to call my parents, *if* I'm going to call my parents.

'I don't know,' I say honestly. 'It all depends, right?' At the very least, I could spare them the waiting and worrying.

At 1 P.M., the phone rings, and Emily Birenbaum says these exact words, 'Kelly, I have the biopsy report and, Kelly, it's cancer.'

I put my hand to my mouth: 'Edward!' and he comes to me and we crowd around the phone, the one in the kitchen that is tethered to the wall, politely asking the simplest of questions. 'Is the test always correct?' 'Does it say how much cancer there is?' 'Could it be a false positive?' We are on our best behavior, as you would be with someone at the airlines who might be able to get you an upgrade. After a short conversation, during which we learn the phrase 'invasive ductal carcinoma,' we hang up. The girls are at our knees,

56

needing to be fed and put down for a nap.

'I want a peanut butter and cream cheese samwich,' Georgia announces.

'What do you say?' The back-and-forth is automatic.

'Pees.'

So out comes the jar, the bread, the cream cheese, the cutting board, the booster seat, the milk, the napkins, the sponge.

'What do you say?'

'Fank you.'

I put the plates down in front of them.

'You're welcome.'

The routine soothes. The kitchen is quiet. I hold on to the edge of the sink with my back to the girls. I can feel Edward coming up behind me.

'I'm sorry,' I say, turning to him and starting to cry. 'You don't deserve this. You're not some kind of absentee father who needs a wake-up call. You shouldn't have to go through this. I'm sorry I'm defective.'

Edward, who is on his game today, takes my hands and wraps them around his waist, and pulls me in, saying, 'Better or worse, Kel, better or worse. I wouldn't trade this defective body for anything.' I hold on tighter and tighter and bawl until Georgia and Claire start to fight because Claire is throwing pieces of her sandwich off her tray and

Georgia is insisting on order.

'Why don't you go out on the deck? I'll get these guys down,' Edward says.

★ ★ ★

As Edward gets the girls settled upstairs, I dial Tracy, then Missy, then MaryHopeSarah-ChadAmieMegAndy until I am warmed up and ready to call my brothers. Edward comes back down, and I hear him in the kitchen, opening beers. He sits across from me on the deck and hands me a Corona with a lime. I put my feet up on his lap, and he holds my ankles. We don't even know each other yet, or so said some long-married friends of ours recently. You'll see, they laughed, you're newlyweds. We're thirty minutes into our first crisis, and so far, we're doing all right. I want to be outside, I want the beer, I want him to hold my ankles, and he seems to know all that.

'What a day,' he says. I nod, even though I'm not sure if he's referring to the diagnosis or the inappropriately blue skies or both. 'How are the calls going?'

'Well, I left messages for Booker and GT. Tracy and Missy burst into tears and Mary Hope is coming over — she'll be here in an hour. Sarah is going to get recommendations

58

on local doctors, and Amie wants to take the girls tomorrow.'

'I'm gonna call my parents,' he says, squeezing my ankles.

'Okay, I'm ready.' I watch him dial. I stare at his mouth, like a lip-reader. I see the words come out. I try to hear what he's saying, but there's a humming, or a dreaminess, to it that softens then blurs.

After we hang up, he opens his laptop and writes an e-mail to his college friends, another to his locals, then his boss, his assistant.

We are troops in motion. We may have argued over the likelihood of war, but now that we've been dropped on enemy soil, marching in formation comes easily, and the synchronicity is so fucking comforting that it makes cancer seem a tenth the beast that fear is.

GT calls back. I tell him to close his office door and sit down. I feel like an actress practicing my lines or a kid doing a book report. I tell him that I have breast cancer, and he asks me if he should come out. I don't know what he should do.

'I'm sorry,' I say, realizing that people will want instructions. 'I guess you could go over to Mom and Dad's house after work, just to check in on them.'

'Sure, of course.'

'I haven't called them yet,' I say. 'I'm practicing on you.'

I can tell he likes this. It makes him feel useful. He will want to be my hero. He will want to make the dramatic appearance, the essential connection, the critical contribution. This is how he loves. He dreams of greatness. We have this in common. The other line clicks. I look at the number.

'Hey, that's Booker on the other line. I'll call you tomorrow, okay?'

'Please,' he implores. 'Or tonight. Whenever you know more.' There is a pause where an 'I love you' would go, but it's too loaded today, and we're not that good at saying it anyway.

Booker immediately turns on his rousing coach-speak, which I bet works great on fourteen-year-olds.

'Kelbo, you can do this! It's like I tell my players — you gotta get out there and do the work. You gotta chip away at it one day at a time. Look at Lance Armstrong. Six yellow jerseys!'

I let him think he's emboldened me, that his battle cry has been heard, even though it just feels like pressure to be more than I am or could ever be.

Booker wants to talk to Edward. Booker and GT love Edward, and this validation is way too important to me. More than once, I'd broken up with a nice boy I actually liked just to avoid introducing him to my brothers, who I knew would eat him alive. The one time I didn't, I still hear about from GT, who likes to tell anyone who will listen about this guy I brought to a Rolling Stones show. He was a dud, but also tall and broad-shouldered, so he came off as mysterious. I thought his silence was concealing something fascinating; I remember staring at him a lot while he slept. Anyway, when GT tells the story, the punch line is 'He was sitting down during 'Start Me Up!' *Sitting down*. There were fifty-nine thousand nine hundred ninety-nine people dancing and one guy, in row *fourteen*, sitting down.' You can't sit down at a Stones show if you want to make it with GT Corrigan. Although Edward is not a huge Stones fan, he knows better than to take a load off during their signature number.

Edward assures Booker that he will 'take care of Kelly,' which sounds kind of solicitous and knightly and that is just fine with me.

I can't avoid Wooded Lane any longer. As I dial, I remind myself of this crazy thing my friend Missy told me about her husband, Rob. He had been in the Marine reserves for twelve years when G. W. Bush invaded Iraq. Rob and Missy had a little boy, who had just started talking and walking, and a brand-new baby girl, twelve weeks old. Even so, Rob couldn't wait for his unit to be called. With uncharacteristic passion, he explained to Missy that this — war — is what he had been training for. He admitted that he had always been disappointed that he missed the action in the first Gulf War. He hoped for placement in Iraq, where he would spend half a year fixing broken water lines and distributing freeze-dried food to lonely, scared guys in hollowed-out buildings, never quite adjusting to the unpredictable rumble of bombs going off in the night, but all the same, finding ways to rebuild infrastructure and restore some order. I know my parents will want to be called into active duty too.

My dad isn't home, he's out playing tennis; my mom says she's on the porch, going through the mail. She rags me for not returning her call last week.

'Oh, well, Mom, um, a lot has been going on out here. I actually — found a lump in my breast last week.' I go slowly, bit by bit. 'So I had a mammogram on Wednesday.' She'll figure out what's going on before I even tell her. 'And a biopsy on Friday.' She knows already. 'And the doctor just called with the pathology report.' Deep breath. 'And — it's cancer.'

'Oh my God, Kelly. Oh my God. When did you find the lump?'

I go back and outline last week for her again, belaboring every episode so she can acclimate to the thinner air. I know her job is to keep me from harm. After all, I am a mother now too. I know what it is to want to safeguard your children. It starts with the first prenatal vitamin and it never ends. Safety gates, life vests, fire drills, swim lessons, CPR. And still, one day, the kid you've been so careful to protect might call to say she has cancer.

I talk. She listens without interruption. When she does rejoin the conversation, she takes a problem-solving posture, enumerating what she'll do on her end and what I should be doing on mine. No tears, no nonsense.

'So,' I interrupt, 'can you get Dad on his cell? Can you have him call me? Are you going to tell him?'

'Yes, honey, I'll call him. I'll tell him. He'll call you as soon as I can track him down. Don't worry. I'll find him.' She knows, as she always has, that I am a little bit more his girl than hers.

With the phone still pressed against my ear, I feel my selves pulling me — frantic child clawing her way out of the doctor's office, then composed adult, competent and steady. This is it. I've finally been slung out of the society of the naive and untested.

An hour later, I hear Edward say, 'She's right here, Big George.' He hands me the phone, and I walk outside. It is dreamlike. Honest to God, I can't hear what he's saying, what outrageous promises he's making, but I know he isn't worried. I know he is deeply convinced that I can handle it.

'Lovey, I gotta believe that a girl as strong as you — ' He pauses, and I am holding my breath. 'I'm just saying, you can do this, Lovey. You're special. I've always said it. You're just a very special girl, that's all.'

He talks about the best doctors and lots of prayers and coming out on the next flight out and I just kept nodding and saying, 'Right, right . . . that's right . . . you're right' and with each word, I get younger and more dependent until I feel like I am small enough to crawl into his lap.

He had been right before. He knew, when I didn't, that California was the right move, that I'd find work, and a man, that children would come. His faith — in God, in the human spirit, in me — had long ago made him impervious to anxiety. It seemed useless to disagree with him. Why *not* believe in the enchanted place where he lives?

★ ★ ★

The next day, between calling doctors and scheduling appointments, I send out this very brave-sounding, very George Corrigan-ish e-mail to about a hundred people:

> **To:** All
> **Date:** August 10, 2004, 6:49 A.M.
> **Re:** Looking Ahead

Hi all,

Brace yourself. Yesterday, I was diagnosed with breast cancer. I'll get you all the details later this week, as I get them, but for now, I wanted to invite you all to a party-to-end-all-parties, August 13, 2005. In just about a year, I will turn 38 with my girls at my side and my husband on my arm and we will toast to the end of a long year. And there will be many thank-yous for a thousand favors and good wishes, and there will be much hugging and kissing. There will be dancing, wild dancing, and people will say stuff like, 'Isn't this what life is all about?' and 'I knew she'd beat it!'

In the meantime, my OB thinks it'll be about six months of chemo, then surgery, then radiation, and then perhaps hormone therapy. This plan leaves no room for error,

65

so we can be confident that the aforementioned party will be the last of its kind.

I have a great team of doctors who are going to make all this go away, and more importantly, I have a great team of people at 455 Mountain, including my parents, Edward, Georgia and Claire, who are going to keep the trains running on time around here.

So far, cancer has meant flowers on my doorstep (already!), family on their way to Piedmont, people saying a bunch of nice shit about me, and tons of long hugs. So who could complain about that?

It's gonna be a great party, next summer.

Kelly

As we're going to sleep, I tell Edward that I sent out a big e-mail. He wants to know why I didn't read it to him first.

'I'm embarrassed,' I say as I close my eyes and settle in.

'Why?'

'You'll see. It's very — upbeat.'

We are learning each other, and what he is discovering about me is that although I am no George Corrigan, I can do a pretty good imitation when I need to.

8

It's good, like a miracle is good, to know that there's somebody who will follow you down whatever path you choose.

By the time I was ten or eleven, it was clear that neither tennis nor lacrosse was going to stick. So I took up the curious sport of diving. Like all pursuits, diving has its own community of diehards who relish the particulars — degree of difficulty, required dives, sticky fulcrums, the dreaded balk. (A balk is when the diver starts moving down the board and then stops. It involves a big penalty, over and above the humiliation.) My parents played right along, using the lingo, buying me a square foot of chamois cloth to dry off like the pros, and taping the swim-meet schedule onto the inside of the pantry door. In the summer of 1976, they gave me temporary control over the television set so I could watch Greg Louganis win a medal in Montreal. Even my brothers had to admit that it was rad to watch a sixteen-year-old jump off a thirty-foot concrete platform and do all those flips and turns.

A lot of swim teams only had one or two

real divers, which meant that some meets, I only had to beat one other person to get first place. Sometimes, that one other person wasn't even a real diver, just a swimmer with a sense of humor who the coach put in to get the second-place points. Although I didn't generally like sports, I did like ribbons and applause, so diving was perfect.

After a summer or two, another girl my age joined the team, a girl with the unlikely name of Emelyn Wampler. By this point, I loved the attention I got from my family, so I practiced every day, once with the coach, and once by myself. I liked to go through my set of six dives at least four times. I'm pretty sure it was the most dogged I've ever been about anything. Too bad it was jumping into a pool.

The better I got, the closer to the board my dives came and the harder it was for my mother to watch. She soothed her nerves by squeezing my dad's forearm and sucking up Benson & Hedges. She could be heard packing a fresh box against her palm before every meet.

Everyone came to my meets, my parents, even my brothers, who probably spent the time categorizing the breasts of the girls on the swim team. But only my dad watched me practice.

He would come down from the tennis

courts at Martin's Dam, our summer swim club, and watch me finish my training routine. He'd unlace his shoes and set his feet free. Then he'd let out a satisfied 'Awww' as he leaned back into a lounge chair, his sweaty hair curling around the top of his white padded visor, and open up his *Sports Illustrated* that he'd been carrying around for just this moment.

'Lovey, take your time. I'll stay as long as you want,' he'd say before picking out his first article. As the sun got lower, he'd put his drugstore sunglasses up on his visor. The pair I remember best had mirror lenses and yellow plastic frames with multicolored edges, like Suzy Chapstick's. Having absolutely no background in diving but for the education I was giving him, he managed to feel expert enough to say things like 'I'll tell you what, Lovey, you better look out for Emelyn Wampler. That gainer of hers is *big time*.'

'Dad, nobody says 'gainer.' It's a reverse,' I corrected him, wringing out my hair and wishing he were less right about Emelyn Wampler.

Emelyn Wampler, who was always referred to by her full name, grew up on this little horse farm, where she had an unusual number of chores for someone our age. She was pretty devoted to diving. She used to make scorecards on her chaise lounge at the pool, tabulating imaginary totals based on scores she thought she could count on from the judges. She used a calculator. When I'd walk by, she'd slide the paper under her thigh and look up at me like she was just doodling and taking in the magnificent day, and hey, did I need some baby oil?

The night after the practice when she became the first person at Martin's Dam to do a layout in reverse, my dad drove me home. I turned to him on the lovely ride home, past soft green fields that have since been sold and subdivided, and said, 'Emelyn Wampler is doing a reverse in layout. It's pretty good. Degree of difficulty: one point nine.'

'Yeah? . . . Sounds like it's time to turn it up a notch. Have you tried it?'

'Scares me. Afraid I'll land on my back.'

'Wanna go back? Pool's open 'til eight. I bet it's a ghost town now.'

'No, Mom'll be pissed.'

'Don't talk like that, Lovey.'

'Sorry.'

'Maybe tomorrow night,' he said, letting me off the hook. 'We'll get that old Emelyn Wampler, Lovey.'

Before I really appreciated what I was bringing on myself, I told him what he wanted to hear, so he'd be proud of my plucky spirit. 'Okay, let's go back. I'll try it — once.' I knew we were so different in this way. I knew he loved sport and competition and going to the next level. I loved other things. I loved him. I loved rearranging my room and styling my hair and pretending I was an ad exec in the upstairs walk-in closet that I had transformed into a faux office. But sometimes, charging him up was enough.

I started by doing a couple of basic reverse dives, loosening my tuck a little more each time until my legs were almost straight. And then, kinda by accident, I ended up in an upside-down jackknife, and from there, I just dropped my chest and arms down toward the water and slipped in.

'How was that?' I said, breaking the seal of the water, knowing the answer already.

'Lovey! Fantastic! Now whaddaya call that? Is that a pike? I love it. It's a killer!'

I was out of the pool now, jumping on one leg to get some water out of my ear, and acting nonchalant. 'Yep. That's a reverse in pike,' I said, trying to hold back a smile. A reverse in pike was something I had never seen anyone do, and it felt very cool and distinguished.

'Fantastic! Emelyn Wampler doesn't have a chance. You gonna do it again?'

'Yep,' I said, opting to skip the stairs and duck under the silver rail to get back on the board. 'You bet I am.'

After five or six more times, I owned it. Thanks to the magic combination of Greenie's bottomless faith in me and my equally bottomless desire to thrill him, Emelyn Wampler was gonna have to run her numbers again.

On the ride home, staring out again at the soft green fields, blue-lipped and wrapped in a maroon towel with my name in big white block letters, I gloried in that weird, good, waterlogged feeling. We didn't talk much, but every now and then my dad would call out enthusiastically, apropos of nothing, 'Love-E!' Didn't matter that diving wasn't his sport. Your kid is your kid, and wherever they take you, you go.

9

My dad is on his way to Oakland, probably clad in his Radnor lacrosse sweats. I am due for my first chemo on Monday morning. With a life driven by sports, sales, and Catholicism, my dad's MO will doubtlessly involve *attacking it, staying positive,* and *having faith.*

I'm not quite there. I've been so grown-up in so many meetings, conversations, and appointments lately. Such a big girl. Such a good girl. With my dad in the house, I am someone's child again. Someone else has to get me an iced tea, make me some dinner, bring me a cookie. Just thinking about how good it's going to be to have him around makes me well up. By the time I spot him on the curb at the airport, I am trembling.

'Aw, Lovey,' he says as he squeezes me and rocks me side to side. 'Love-E! We're gonna do it, kid. We're gonna get it done. The Green Man is here, Lovey.' I hold on a long time, crying and whispering 'yeah' over and over again.

When we come through the front door,

73

Edward is waiting for us. They hug a nice loud man hug.

'Green Man, thanks for coming, man,' Edward says while they pat each other on the back.

'ARK!' my dad says. 'Ark, God bless you.' My dad named Edward 'Arkansas Ed' before he even met him, when he was just a guy who took me to a concert. In less than a year, Arkansas Ed became Ark, sometimes even Arkie.

'Come on in, Greenie. I'll take that.' Edward runs the suitcase upstairs. 'Green Man,' he calls from the second floor, 'I got some Ketel One for you.'

'Whoa! Ark! Top shelf! Fantastic. How 'bout I start with a beer, though . . . ' My dad is talking into the fridge, searching out a cold beer, something to ease him into the vodka. I am smiling. Edward is down the stairs in no time. The girls are at Amie's for dinner.

'Greenie, I got you some Bud Lights. You know, we usually have that heavy California beer, but I know you Philly guys love a Bud so . . . ' My dad pulls out a can of beer and opens one for Edward and raises his eyebrow at me and I nod and he hands me his and leans in the fridge for another and there we are, just like any other visit, having a cold beer together.

74

'Big day on Monday.' I try to say it like my dad would, like it's a lacrosse game or a job interview. But I am not Greenie, and I start crying.

'Lovey,' he says as he runs his big, rough hand in circles on my rounded back, 'you gotta stay positive. Right, Ark? We gotta stay positive.'

I want to wail like Georgia did last week when she slipped in the bathroom and hit her head on the tub, enraged, writhing, then sniveling into Edward's shoulder, leaving a big wet spot of tears and snot on his work shirt.

But right then, with his hand still going in circles on my back, my dad says, 'Now, Ark, tell me about Johnny Depp — is he the real deal? Am I supposed to take him seriously?' And Edward tells him yes, he is definitely the real deal, and they talk a little about Johnny Depp movies until they can't remember what movie he is in right now and I actually hear myself say *Pirates of the Caribbean* and they say 'Right, right, that's it.'

It's the same trick we use when the girls start skidding into despair. 'Oh sweetie, don't cry, we'll find your bunny slipper, oh LOOK!' we say in buoyant preschool-teacher voices. 'Look at Mr. Piggy! He's all alone in the living room. You better go give Piggy a hug . . .'

I sleep better that night, partly because I take two Ambien instead of one, and partly because Greenie is here, padding around in his Brooks Brothers pajamas, delighting the girls by letting them watch him pop out his dentures and promising to let Georgia paint his toenails the next day.

* * *

Over a breakfast of coffee and chocolate chip cookies, I ask Greenie if he's ever had a pedicure. He laughs because his toenails are prehistoric — as grainy as petrified wood. I love pedicures, but I am too cheap to get them. I want him to treat me to one. That, and I'm kinda starved for his particular energy, so I want him to come along.

'You gonna leave the girls here with Ark? Ark, you okay with that?' my dad asks, which of course Edward is, because you can have anything you want when you have cancer, especially in the beginning.

'Of course,' Edward says.

'Sounds great to me, Lovey! Can we take the Peach in there?' he asks, overestimating the capacity of a three-year-old to sit still.

'No, not yet.'

We drive down College Avenue toward Berkeley and pull up to Galaxy Nails, where they have an empty row of massage chairs. The door's been propped open with a little foam wedge of pink toenail separators. The Korean sisters who run the place wave us in. We climb up into our thrones, and I explain to Greenie how to use the chair controls — rolling thunder, beating hands, ocean waves.

'Lovey! Fantastic!' Then he looks toward the sisters. 'Ladies, I'm just an old Billy Goat out for my first pedicure!' He settles in like a regular, with the *New York Times* on his lap. I try to warn the sisters about his toenails, but words become unnecessary as he slides his crooked feet out of his updated Docksiders that have molded to the shape of his feet. Two of his toes are taped together with white athletic tape — and have been for years. One of the sisters rolls up his pant leg and guides his feet into the churning warm water, and he lets out a long sigh. His contentedness spreads. We are all happy.

★ ★ ★

That evening, Edward is barbecuing pork tenderloins and I am drinking too much, because drinking feels so good. Everything is funnier, less pointy and sharp. Our friends Deryl and Allison Seale are over, and we're talking about my treatment plan like I've had cancer for years and we all know the routine. After dinner, we laze around the living room on our worn-out IKEA sofas, and I drink more red wine, and my eyes are bloodshot; I'm listening to my husband and Deryl play guitar. My dad wants to hear 'Sweet Caroline' and even though they don't know the chords, they wing it, and Greenie sings the words he can remember in whatever order they come to him and Edward is laughing with Deryl. Georgia is in her zip-up fleece pajamas with the baggy bottom and she wants to hear her favorite song, which is Deryl and Edward's best one: 'The Only Living Boy in New York.' We've gone through two bottles of wine already but I notice my dad open another red without even asking if anyone wants more. It occurs to me that this sort of thing may be what alcohol is for — dulling, soothing consolation. He refills everyone while Edward and Deryl play for Georgia. She won't sing out loud, but she stares at her dad's face as he sings, and her lips move to the words. She adores him. Then Allison suggests this old song by the guy from Little Feat called 'Roll Um Easy.' It's the first song I ever heard Edward play. When he gets to the line I like, he looks across at me with his pinchy guitar-playing face and nods to me:

I have dined in palaces,
Drunk wine with Kings and Queens,
But darlin', oh darlin,'
You're the best thing I ever seen.

I shift my position on the sofa, so my head is on a big, lumpy pillow in Greenie's lap and Georgia is leaning back against my middle and Claire is just about asleep on the floor. Allison and I catch eyes, and she tilts her head and smiles, and when I smile back, we both well up with tears, I think because we both recognize that whatever else may be unfolding, this is happiness.

10

All things considered, I'd rather have warning that something bad was coming than have it hit me from behind. Sixth grade knocked me to my knees, especially since it followed fifth grade, which had gone so well.

In fifth grade, my best friend ever, Allison Mundth, and I had the world by the tail. We split our time between drawing contests and creating exclusive clubs for ourselves. Sometimes, a drawing, say of a crown and scepter, became part of a club logo, which went on top of club stationery, which was used for all club communications, including club elections.

But then John Tucker and Chris Kerlin came along, and it was time to deal with the inevitable. The first problem was how to sort out who should go out with whom. To figure it out, Allison wrote John Tucker's name in capital letters above mine, circled all the mutual consonants, then applied a complex algorithm. John and I scored a thirty-seven, which meant we were destined to be married and, moreover, that our union would generate thirteen children. So Allison got Chris Kerlin.

Other than all the math, fifth grade boyfriends weren't much trouble. John and I barely talked and were not expected to hold hands. Kissing was years off. But if either of my brothers were to come upon a careless doodle — like KC + JT, 2gether, 4ever, 6cess — well, that could ruin my life. Consequently, my notebooks were covered with patches of deep, black scribbles.

I started middle school feeling optimistic. My class was made up of the graduates of three local elementary schools, including a parochial school. You'd think those Catholic school kids would be extra nice, having had the benefit of the Bible and the nuns and all, but you'd be wrong. In fact, one of them — their leader — was, as I overheard my mom say, *a goddamn rotten egg.*

Her name was Claudia, and in the early weeks of the school year, she vigorously befriended both Allison and me, inviting us for a sleepover at her huge house, which was even bigger than Allison's, which was twice the size of 168 Wooded Lane. Also unlike my house, Claudia's had a walk-in pantry full of sugared cereals. You could have an overflowing bowl of Lucky Charms, followed by Crunchberries sprinkled with Frosted Flakes, and still have more options the next morning. Allison kept her cool around all this largesse, but I found it impossible not to ask if I couldn't have a quick bowl of Honeycombs before we went upstairs to Claudia's room. I knew it was a mistake when Claudia handed me a spoon and then said to Allison, 'I usually eat cereal in the morning. There's ice cream sandwiches in the garage freezer. Want one?'

After they got back from their snack, we headed up to Claudia's room. Although she was more of a tomboy than a glamour puss, Claudia did have a Gatsby-esque sweater collection. Turtlenecks, cable-knits, cardigans with metal buttons as detailed as a coat of arms. I was too impressed. Surrounded by Fair Isles of every color, we turned to the work of the night: dividing up the boys in our class into three categories: Just Okay, Grody, Total Foxes. Even considering my amateurish move with the Honeycombs, the night went well enough. I thought.

But a little while after the sleepover — the much-bragged-about, oft-referred-to sleepover — Claudia started passing notes to Allison in chorus. And calling her every night. And twisting open Oreos with her at lunch. I don't know exactly why Claudia picked Allison instead of me, but I hated having to compete for Allison's attention, something I had enjoyed unchallenged for years.

Not too long after the notes and calls and Oreos started, our group of girls starting having what were called Truth Circles, during which ten or twelve girls sat in a circle and told the truth. For example, 'The zit on your neck is totally disgusting,' 'Your hair is kinda greasy,' or my favorite, 'You wear your pants too high.' It was positioned as something friends should do, as in 'I am your friend and only a friend would care enough to tell you that those overalls give you a wedgie, in the front.' One day, toward the very end of recess, Claudia looked at me across the circle and said, 'Your teeth are as big as horse teeth.' Several people nodded, my stomach dropped out, and Claudia added, 'Maybe you just shouldn't show your teeth so much when you smile.' The buzzer went off and the circle dispersed. As I walked to social studies with my lips wrapped around my teeth, I overheard Claudia say to Allison, 'Omigod no! *Your* teeth are perfect . . . ' This was worse than having brothers.

That night, I told my dad the story. He chuckled and said something about how his brothers used to call him Bucky Beaver, and right then, my brothers blew through the kitchen, breaking each other up with cracks like, 'You just gotta *buck* up, Kel!' and 'Hey Kel, wanna watch *Leave It to Beaver?*' I stormed upstairs and told my mom what Claudia said and I could see her set her jaw in anger. Finally, somebody was feeling my pain. Then she forced a smile and said, 'Your teeth are beautiful. You have a perfect smile. Don't you listen to that little' — she paused — 'girl.'

Things at school continued to deteriorate. There was a slumber party at Claudia's that I didn't know about until Claudia called my house and held out the phone on her end into a cluster of hysterical girls. That night, my parents talked about it in their room. I couldn't hear their words but the tone of my mother's voice made it clear that to cross me was to cross her.

A month later, I got a hot pink party invite from Jodi Leaming. She was a sweet girl, nonpartisan. My mom pinned the invite to the bulletin board, and every time I passed it, I felt a little rush of pride. I mentioned it to my brothers once or twice, as in, 'Well, I won't be here for dinner on Friday because I have a party to go to.' My dad said he could drive me over. Then, the night before, Claudia called to tell me that Jodi didn't really want me to come but her mom told her she had to invite me.

'What should I do?' I cried to my mom.

'Maybe you should go wearing pads and a

helmet,' GT said, laughing.

'What?' I asked, knowing I was being teased but not knowing how.

'So when they start using you as a punching bag, you won't get bruises,' Booker said.

'Mom!'

'That's enough, you two,' she said in a threatening tone. 'Go outside or upstairs or to the basement. Now.'

She could barely protect me from my brothers; how could she hope to protect me from sixth grade politics?

I didn't go to the party. I didn't have the heart to risk it, and my mom didn't have the heart to make me.

* * *

There were more Truth Circles, and although my mother implored me to walk away from them, I just couldn't. 'The mole right near your eye looks like a giant wart,' Claudia shared with me one day.

I often came down Wooded Lane in tears of frustration. My mom ran out of upbeat things to say, having blown through the obvious — 'Who needs her anyway?' and 'We certainly won't invite her to *your* party!' — by Thanksgiving. By the time summer came, I

85

was shaky and self-conscious. Going back to school seemed suicidal.

But in the fall of seventh grade, Claudia was called to the principal's office. She had tied a girl to a chain-link fence using the strings of the girl's yellow smock sundress. It took a teacher ten minutes to undo the knots. I can still see that girl's blotchy face and pimply shoulders. This put an end to the Truth Circles, as teachers were on the lookout for any activity Claudia seemed to be coordinating. And a few boys made it known that they thought Claudia had gone too far. Breasts, which Claudia did not have, were becoming more important. Whatever the reason, Allison and I went back to doing more things together, just us. Claudia's dominance was waning.

Then things broke for good in eighth grade when word got around that Andy Sheehan had a crush on me. Andy Sheehan was the pick of the litter, confirmed later that spring by the Radnor Middle School yearbook, which named him 'Most Popular' *and* 'Cutest Boy.' I considered his affections, along with having the braces removed from my giant teeth, divine intervention. I only had to make it to the last day of middle school, since the next year, Claudia would go to an all-girls Catholic school and I would be safe at

Radnor High, Andy Sheehan by my side and my sporty, surefooted brothers just down the hall. Graduation marked the end; I had survived.

* * *

One summer between college years, I was out on the deck at Wooded Lane having some Inglenook over ice with my mom, probably smoking one of her extra-long Benson & Hedges, which she had begun sharing with me when I turned twenty. I asked her what the worst time in her life was.

'Sixth grade was pretty bad,' she said, thinking out loud.

'Wow, me too.'

'Not my sixth grade, Kelly. *Your* sixth grade.'

'Why?' I asked, wondering if I had forgotten something terrible that had happened to her that year.

'You'll see. When you're a mother and your kid's in pain and you can't stop it — it's hell. Absolute hell.'

11

The sounds of the Infusion Center are hushed and infrequent, like the first-class cabin on an airplane. Some patients are reclined in their chairs, sleeping away the time. Others knit or read the paper. A professional woman next to me types lightly on her laptop, not letting anything interfere with her deadlines. Nurses bring juice and blankets like flight attendants, whose purpose is to keep you safe but whose time is generally spent keeping you comfortable.

Catherine, a soft-spoken, no-nonsense nurse with a sudden smile, punctures my skin and the IV is in. No heat, no chill, no tingling. The first bag is saline, then a bag of Zofran, an antinausea medication, and then I'm ready to get what I came for: chemotherapy. Catherine shows me a plunger as wide and long as a turkey baster. The medicine itself is red, like cherry Kool-Aid.

'This is the Adriamycin. It's pretty powerful, so we administer it by hand, slowly,' she says. 'Tell me if you feel hot or flush.'

I watch the IV line turn red. Georgia would love this. It's like playing doctor.

'Do you feel okay?' Catherine asks as she surveys me.

'Fine,' I report. 'So, I get four doses of this?'

'That's right. Just four.'

'No matter what? I mean, no matter what the tumor does?' I'm thinking if it is really working, why not give me more?

'They don't like you to have more than four doses.'

'Why?'

'It's hard on your heart,' she says.

'So, even if I get cancer again, even in twenty years, they can't put me back on it?'

'Probably not.'

Edward and I exchange glances. I remember a conversation I overheard once when my uncle Tommy was sick. My mom had been down in Baltimore with him, and she came through the back door fuming.

'That damn chemotherapy is practically killing him,' she said to my dad.

'I think that's how it works, sweetheart. I think it *just about* kills you.'

'God, George, I don't know how he stands it. Honestly. I don't know how he stands it,' she said, leaning on the counter.

'He's strong, Mare. I'll go down there next week and sit with him,' he said, rubbing her back in circles like he does. Then, after a minute, he had an idea. 'How 'bout we go to eleven-fifteen mass? Whaddaya say?'

Some people go to bed, some go for a run, others go to the refrigerator. When my parents need escape or comfort, they go to God's house.

'Lemme change my shoes,' my mom said, since going to church in the wrong shoes practically negated the impact of going to church at all.

★ ★ ★

'Now, this is the Cytoxan,' Catherine says as she hangs a clear plastic bag on the hook.

People don't just fall into oncology, like they might banking or insurance. I want to know more about Catherine, why she's here and how much she understands about us, the patients. Plus, I'm hoping to become the teacher's pet so she'll always give me a good seat, double-check the label on the IV bag, and be gentle with the needles.

'Do you have kids?' I ask. I want her to know that I do. Two little kids who need me to last a long time.

'Three — two boys and a girl. You?'

After some of the usual chatter mothers can have a thousand times and somehow still mean it — about kids and how hard it is, how fast it goes, how much they change you — I ask Catherine how she came to work here. She said she always wanted to be a nurse. I ask if her mom was a nurse. She says no and then, after a pause, she says her mom was a patient. I ask if she had cancer. She nods. I ask if it was breast cancer. She nods again as she watches the Cytoxan slide through the line. I ask if she got good treatment. She says she died when Catherine was six. I say oh, God, and ask her how her dad managed. She says he died a year and a half later. She surveys me again for early signs of an allergic reaction to the medications. I ask her who took care of her. She says she went to live with her aunt, along with her brother and sister. I ask if any of them have had cancer. She says no as she peels off the blue rubber gloves that protect her from the medication and me from infection. I ask if she's had the test, to see if she has the gene, the gene that nearly guarantees you will have breast cancer. She shakes her head. 'Don't wanna know.' She adds that it's funny we're talking about this because no one at the Infusion Center knows about her mom. No one here knows that her career and her humility come from a woman she barely remembers, who died thirty-odd years ago.

'Okay, you're set,' Catherine says, punching some numbers into the IV machine. 'You've got about two and a half hours of Cytoxan. If you have to use the bathroom, you can unplug the machine and roll it in there with you. It flips over to the battery automatically.'

'Got it,' I say.

'Are you warm enough? We have blankets. We also have tea, and juice, and graham crackers.'

It's like snack and nap time all at once. She has the perfect touch, Catherine. Respectful, conscientious, but routine all the same. Edward likes her too. After she leaves, we congratulate ourselves on getting 'the good one,' and Edward says if I want, he'll talk to the front desk and make sure I always get her.

'Yeah, definitely,' I say.

Edward pulls out the New Yorker he's working on and I find my place in the latest David Sedaris book. We interrupt each other every so often to read a line aloud.

Between stories, I take in the woman across from me. She looks like she's come into the big city from her farm in Central California — they don't sell shoes like hers in the city. She looks about fifty. Her IV bag is bulging; she has hours to go. She keeps glancing over at me and smiling, like she wants to talk, like the people on planes who want to make friends in the air. Her skin is pale and gray even though it's August and her eyebrows are gone. She's a regular. Maybe she knows something I should know, like home remedies for nausea. Or maybe she'll try to foist something on me, like soy milk or knitting, or Jesus.

'Is this your first day?' she asks, after I linger on her too long.

'Yeah, my maiden voyage.'

Without much provocation, she tells me in her librarian voice about how much weight she's lost, mostly because of mouth sores, which make eating uncomfortable, and which bleed sometimes, and also because many of her favorite foods now taste rancid to her. She tells us how chemo alters the receptor cells in your mouth. I am engrossed.

I can feel Edward's foot pressing on mine. I know he doesn't want me to hear any more. He wants me to go back to my funny book and he wants this woman to stop telling her bad-news sob story. But I can't resist. I ask about other side effects, which she readily recounts. Pain in her feet, numb fingers, both of which usually go away after several months, but sometimes they're permanent, she says with some pride. Cramping, diarrhea, forgetfulness — it's like she's reaching into a wicker basket and tossing out snakes.

'Hi, Mary,' Catherine says, coming back to check on me.

'Hello,' Mary says.

Catherine leans into my machine and says quietly, 'Everybody responds to chemo differently. Mary has more complaints than most.'

'And Kelly's so young,' Edward says, looking to Catherine for confirmation.

'That's right,' Catherine says to us. Then she turns around to address Mary. 'You're not scaring my new patient are you?' she says, winking like she's just kidding.

Then she shows me how to make my chair recline.

★   ★   ★

After four hours, I am deflowered. We say our good-byes, admit to each other in the elevator that it wasn't that bad, dig out eighteen dollars for parking, and head home to see the girls before they go to bed. Bay Bridge traffic has other plans for us. By the time we pull up to the house, it's dark outside. We eat dinner with Greenie, a sausage and pasta meal that a friend dropped off that afternoon. My dad says he's proud of me. He tells me about the girls, how good, how funny, how easy they were all day. I tell him about Catherine the orphan, which gets us talking about things I inherited from him.

'I guess you probably got *the cancer thing* from my side, so thank God we also gave you good skin, thick hair, and a sense of humor or you'd probably be ready to sue, huh?'

I note a few things I didn't get: athleticism, unflappableness, faith.

He says I shouldn't worry about that. He's got enough faith for both of us.

The next day is Georgia's preschool orientation picnic. I stay in bed, sleepy from the antinausea medication and still a little queasy, trying to read but not able to quiet my internal dialogue. Once, twice, three times, I drop my book and stare at the ceiling. I hear later that Georgia went outside to cry on a bench by herself because she missed her mommy. Next week is her first big week, and I'll probably still be underwater, swimming up through the murk of nausea, slipping in and out of Vicodin and Ativan and Ambien. She is a good girl who will be fine, but I wish it were me picking her up and hearing that first winded report of the turtle at school or the girl who got in trouble for hitting. Didn't I earn that by being here with her every day of the last three years? Aren't her rites of passage mine too?

12

My first prom, and I didn't even mention it to my mom. I was probably punishing her for something — like giving me a new can of tennis balls for my birthday. Or maybe I was still stewing about how she opened my diary and then, when I walked in on her, pretended she mistook it for my humanities notebook. Whatever the rub, I didn't tell her that Brody McShane had asked me to the junior prom. She found out from Booker, who came home from lacrosse practice appalled by the news, which he'd heard in the locker room. After all, it was technically Booker's prom. I was only a freshman, one who barely taxed a training bra and sometimes still wore OshKosh B'Gosh overalls.

It couldn't have been easy for my mom. Just sorting out my outfit sparked a week's worth of fights, made more dramatic by the release of *Terms of Endearment*, which raised mother-daughter turmoil to an art form. I was easily influenced by cinema and song and soap operas, which inspired some of my best lines, stuff like 'This is not love, Mother. Love doesn't feel this bad.' Then there were the rumors of flasks in tux pockets and bubble kegs in the hotel parking lot. Add to that my mother's concern for my maidenhood and you've got one long month of nail biting, arguing, and aggravation.

In her favor was that Brody McShane was a nerd, an alpha nerd. But what she feared was that I might be the kind of girl to trade up once I got to the dance and did a couple of compulsory rounds on Brody's arm. I would have been easy plucking for some of the dirtier guys — the real veterans — in Booker's class. My mom hinted at her concern by finding several opportunities in the weeks leading up to the prom to say, 'Remember, Kelly, you are there to dance with your date.'

'I KNOW, Mom!' I said, as if I had never yielded to an opportunistic impulse, as if I couldn't decide if the suggestion was more shocking or offensive.

'I'm just saying a lady always leaves with the man who brought her.'

'Mom! Stop!' I whined.

'I'll make sure she behaves,' offered GT.

'What, are you gonna chaperone?' I asked.

'Didn't you hear? Debbie Graves asked me to be her date.'

'Oh my God. This is a nightmare,' I said, unwittingly speaking for both me and my mother, who probably wouldn't have been able to conjure up a more unnerving image than all three of her kids loose at a prom and its after-parties.

Booker came in the back door.

'Hey, Book, you wanna carpool to the prom? Debbie Graves asked me after school today.'

'Oh my God, this sucks,' Booker said inside a giant sigh, making the whole sentence sound like an exhale.

'Scott Corrigan, you know I don't like that word,' my mom scolded.

So all three of us were going to Booker's prom.

My dad was in charge of tuxing up my brothers, which meant a trip out to Betty Moran's house. Betty Moran was, and still is, a person who never met a problem she didn't want to solve. She had three boys who were well out of high school and, consequently, more than a few outgrown tuxedos. Neither my dad nor my brothers were a bit embarrassed to be plumbing her sons' closets for something to wear.

On the other hand, although Betty Moran's princess-beautiful daughter, whom we all called Poopsie, was my age and my size, my mom insisted that I have my own dress. After all, it was my first prom. On the way to the mall, when my mom asked me what I thought a dress would cost, I said that some girls were spending a hundred dollars.

'For a dress they'll never wear again? That's ridiculous,' she said, looking like she'd just sniffed bad cottage cheese. 'I was thinking twenty dollars.'

So instead of borrowing one of Poopsie Moran's dreamy taffeta ballgowns, I was being treated to a new dress. Anything I wanted, for twenty dollars or less.

The winner was a Gunne Sax knockoff that borrowed some of its style from the Puritans and the rest from the Victorians. Full and floor length, the top had fussy floral sleeves and many prudish satin ribbons sewn into a repeating V pattern. The master stroke was the 'collar.' White lace covered my neck completely, coming strangely close to my jawline. I could touch my ear to the lace if I tilted my head a little to one side. When I objected to its primness, my mom convinced me that I wanted a dress that 'left something to the imagination.'

On the afternoon of the prom, my brothers went to pick up their corsages and my bouton-nière, leaving me to obsess over my appearance without interruption or running commentary. I bathed in about a foot of bubbles, wondering what Amy Carter or, better, Caroline Kennedy, did in preparation for her prom. Playing the part in one of my mom's fraying robes, I surrounded myself with the indispensable instruments of hair design; a small pair of very sharp scissors, tortoiseshell Goody hair-pins, Allison Mundth's state-of-the-art curling iron. With a fresh bottle of Final Net, anything was possible.

I parted my hair pristinely down the middle, into two equal halves, leaving my bangs out in front, temporarily clipped together so as to keep them completely isolated. I then used a slightly wet comb to collect the hair on the left side into a tight ponytail, on hold for now. I would start on the right side, my best side, the side with the mole near my eye. My creative vision was twenty-twenty on this one. I knew the success of the design hung on my ability to keep the three parts clean and separate. I bent over, flipping the loose hair on the right side over my head, and started a flawless French braid at the nape of my neck. When I got to just over my ear, I stopped bringing in new hair and finished off the braid, securing it with one of the tiny rubber bands GT was required to wrap around his braces at night. Then I did a very short French braid starting at my crown, not interfering with the bangs, to that same spot over my ear. Now, if you can imagine, I had opposite French braids coming together over my ear, which I pinned into immaculate, concentric circles like Princess Leia, but more dazzling.

I achieved a mirror effect on the left side, given several restarts, and then, after a controlled trim, I carefully used Allison's curling iron to form a hot-dog-roll effect with my bangs. *Voilà!* A couple — ten — pumps of Final Net and it was locked into place. I was ready to lift my ridiculous dress over my hips and hang it on my shoulders. My mom would close me up, using a zipper poorly hidden behind a row of plastic faux-pearl 'buttons.'

This primping session, even for my first prom, tested my mom's patience. My mom had always been concerned that hair might become more than a hobby for me. She had higher hopes — reading maybe, or sewing. Many times on a sunny day when I should have been outside playing, I'd been caught in the blue bathroom that I shared with my disgusting brothers, slavishly working on my hair. When my dad found me in there, newly cut hair around my feet, his only remark was 'Lovey, it's a sunny day! You gotta get outside! Breathe some fresh air! I'm not raising a bunch of hothouse flowers!' but my particular pastime didn't concern him. I could have been in there reading *King Lear* and he'd have said the same thing. He was a great believer in getting outside on a nice day. So I'd open a window and assure him that I was almost finished.

My mom had had the same haircut since before I was born, and any variation in hair color was a mistake or the unfortunate result of her 'colorist's' tendency toward colds in the winter. Coloring your hair was not a choice, my mother would say if you asked her, it was another tiring requirement of ladyhood, like sanitary napkins and suntan panty hose in the summer.

For the record, over the course of the night, I stuck by Brody McShane, even though he brought me a bulky red rose corsage that looked like a gunshot wound pinned onto my dusty peach dress. Without ever making eye contact, we danced dutifully to Devo and Juice Newton and Eddie Rabbitt. My mood changed perceptibly when they played 'Jesse's Girl.' Rick Springfield, in addition to his crackerjack musicianship, played Noah Drake on *General Hospital*. I loved Dr. Drake despite his seedy affair with a breasty, baby-talking hooker turned nurse. Hidden in the low lighting of the Hilton Ballroom, I sang every word, with considerable feeling. Fortunately, Brody was watching his hands bang out chords on his air guitar. It was a dork's Eden. If my brothers had seen me, it would've been tenfold the disgrace of JT + KC, 2gether, 4ever, 6cess. But as usual, they weren't looking at me; I was looking at them.

When they played Grandmaster Flash — the song that sampled 'Another One Bites the Dust' and 'Good Times' — Booker started break-dancing in the middle of a circle of gyrating, overdressed teenagers. The crowd was either doubled over laughing or screaming 'Get it Booker! Oh yeah, Booker!' When Booker came to a stop with his chin resting theatrically in his hand, GT stepped into the center to help him up. They double high-fived. Before the moment ended, Booker looked over and pointed at me, and I beamed like a kid who just got pulled onstage to be the magician's assistant.

Later, during 'Bette Davis Eyes,' Booker was making out with his date, and every time Brody and I turned a full circle, I strained to study Booker's technique. His eyes were pressed shut. His jaw was opening and closing to the beat, like a hungry goldfish who kept time. The kissing went on forever, even past the last note. My own lips stayed dry, as Brody McShane spared me completely. I think at the end of the night, we just looked at each other, shrugged our shoulders, and said 'Bye' with a little hand wave.

The next morning, I heard GT downstairs, dismissing my mom's misplaced concerns. 'She was fine, Mom. I had my eye on her the whole time.'

I could practically hear my mother exhale. 'Well, good, GT. That's very good. That's just what an older brother is supposed to do.'

'Mom, Kelly's not a hose bag,' Booker added.

'Scott Corrigan, you know I don't like that word.'

I was stunned. After years of tattling and torturing, GT had my back, and Booker was right behind him. Without so much as a word between us, my relationship with my brothers had mellowed from combatants to compatriots. That's what I remember most. That, and just how long it took to melt the hairspray off my French braids.

13

friday,
september 10

'Are you surprised that I haven't lost my hair yet?' I ask the oncologist.

'It doesn't happen right away.'

'So it's gonna come out? All of it?'

'Oh definitely. You will lose all your hair,' he confirms.

'Everywhere?' I double-check.

'Everywhere.'

'My eyelashes?'

'Yes.'

'My pubic hair?'

'All of it.'

I know all this, but some things you need to hear a few times before they sink in.

'My girls — if I'm bald — *when* — they'll be so wigged out.'

The doctor walks us over to Susan Marks's office. Susan is a psychologist. Because I wanted to impress her, a professional who might validate my mental health, I say, 'Our biggest concern is how my baldness might affect our children . . . '

105

Susan says that until children turn eight, they can't help but insert themselves into everything. In the absence of something they can see or understand, they make things up. So in this case, my hair falling out is either their fault, or it is going to happen to them next, or both. Maybe I went bald because Claire took the dust jackets off all the books in my office, again, or a shark, like the one in *Finding Nemo*, swam up the stairs and chewed off all my hair. They fabricate stories, Susan explains, because it's easier to share space with something fiendish but defined than something shapeless, just there, in the dark. I nod, remembering how much better it felt to be diagnosed than to be squinting into the glare of possibility, unable to see anything clearly, but sensing its enormity.

So, one evening in early September, my friend Sarah shaves my head out on the deck while the girls watch. Phoebe, Edward's little sister, is here, memorializing the event with a 35mm and helping to create an air of performance. Georgia makes little mustaches out of the hair around my feet. Edward puts a pile of dark brown locks on Claire's head. I drink several whiskey sours and enjoy feelings of liberation and bravery. I am doing it.

But alone in the shower, rubbing tiny hairs off my neck and ears, staring at myself in Edward's shaving mirror suctioned to the wall, it's like an arrow has flown through an open window and hit me in the chest and I can do nothing but hold the arrow and watch the blood dripping from me, over my belly, down my legs, and onto the shower floor, pink and fast-moving in the rush of water, slowly appreciating that this bloodletting will kill me eventually, unless someone finds me there and saves me.

Edward bounds in and opens the shower door and looks at me like he's a teenager seeing tits for the first time.

'I know you're gonna think I'm blowing sunshine up your ass but it looks really good.' I start crying, almost heaving, and he keeps going. 'Really . . . I'm serious . . . you can do this . . . because you have such a pretty face.'

I step out of the running shower to hug him, and to be hugged, and to wail. After a minute, I pull back and hold his shoulders, like a dying matriarch who only has a few words left and must get through. 'I am so proud of you, Edward. You are such a good husband, and that is such an important thing to be, and so many people aren't good at it and you really are. You really are.'

This, like the day I was diagnosed, turns

out to be a great day, a day to remember, a day when we lived up to ourselves and all our promises to each other.

★ ★ ★

It takes several days for me to leave the house. Days, and a final decision about what to wear — hat, turban, bandana, wig. Ears tucked in, now out, now half in. I decide on this certain scarf as my best look, but my usual hoop earrings now bring to mind a fortune-teller, so I switch to silver studs, I guess for the rest of the year. My scarf is pink and white Thai silk, the kind with the little bumps and knots in it, and bits of blue run through the thin stripe pattern. I stand there taking myself in, reconciling it all.

Do I dare drive Georgia to school? Might I even have the nerve to pick up her little friend? Am I a mother again?

'Hey, Lori,' I say, when my friend picks up the phone. 'You know, I think I'm ready to take my look on the road. I think I'll take the kids in today.' She is impressed.

I am in my old Levi's and a white button-down of Greenie's. I look in the mirror more times than I have in a week. My scarf is clinging nicely to itself. A little touch of lip color, much mascara, and I am feeling

108

strangely attractive. Georgia and Claire are in car seats and I am pulling into Lori's driveway right on time.

'Hey, you look beautiful,' says Lori, whose mother happened to die of breast cancer when Lori was in college.

'Yeah? Good. It's not bad, really,' I say, stroking my head like a proud hairdresser.

'Jack! Let's go. Kelly's here!' Lori calls.

Jack comes bouncing down the stairs in a Dora the Explorer T-shirt and jeans and says without any emotion, 'You look like a monster.' Then he glides past me into the den while I stand there speechless.

'Jack!' Lori says, and then looks at me. 'He just saw the movie. Have you seen it? *Monsters, Inc.*?'

I haven't, but I think that's the one with the monster whose bald head looks like a giant eyeball.

'Oh. Um, you know, I think, um,' I say, wishing I had stayed at home where I felt good, 'maybe this isn't a smart idea. I mean, the other kids — '

'Oh, Kelly. Do you want me to take them?'

'Yeah, here,' I say, putting my keys in her hand. 'The girls are in the car. Yeah. I'll be at home.'

I walk out to the driveway, leaving the door open behind me. I tell my girls that Lori

109

wants to drive today, so she's going to take them to school in our car, and won't that be extra fun?

'Let's go, Jack. Right now!' Lori is right behind me, so I turn and walk home, hoping no one I know drives by.

I grab the phone on the way in the door and dial Edward.

'Kel?'

'He called me a monster,' I say, crying and falling into the sofa.

'Who did?'

'Jack Lindgren.'

'That little fucker!'

I don't know what to say about a man who calls a perfectly adorable three-year-old a fucker, but 'my hero' comes to mind.

14

Even when he said no, my dad was an easy flip. All it took was a lot of smiles, a head tilt, and a minor concession of some sort, like doing homework early or taking out a bag of trash. Consequently, I learned to wait until Greenie got home from work to discuss the ten dollars I needed for a new Pappagallo bag or the upcoming unchaperoned pool party at Anne Nealis's. But after one too many 'Sure, why nots?,' my dad learned to stick to the script: 'It's up to your mother.' Unlike Greenie, when my mom took a stand, which she often did, I don't remember her ever backing down. Her fortitude looks like love to me now, but at the time, I was sure my mom was trying to ruin my life.

As I've explained, my mom was formidable on points of fashion, hair, and makeup. But she really dug in her heels when it came to cars. It was her near-pathological anxiety about driving at night that led to The Guess Jeans Fight of 1984.

That fall, when I was a senior in high school, Denise Warner drove me to school every day in a car she bought with wages she had saved from her job at Thrift Drugs, the one next to the Acme in Wayne. Not only did she have her own car, a 'vintage' Dodge Dart, but she also had a stockpile of Guess jeans — black ones, white ones, striped ones. (Do you even know how many pairs you have to have before you start buying patterns?) Suffice it to say, Denise Warner was probably the first girl in the United States to have stonewashed Guess jeans when they debuted a few years later.

Day after day, I tried to come up with a more persuasive way to get my raised-by-Depression-survivors mother to cough up $52 plus tax for one lousy pair of Guess jeans. That was all I needed. With that upside-down red-triangle on my ass, I could do anything. Like, hello RHS Homecoming Court.

'You have two pair of jeans already, Kelly. Perfectly good jeans with no patches,' my mom said, like we lived in Frank McCourt's Limerick and should be thankful that in high school, we weren't wearing Toughskins with iron-on patches over the knees.

It seemed hopeless until one day, while buying three pairs of socks for $8 at The Limited, I saw a framed HELP WANTED notice on the checkout counter.

On the way home, I calculated that at

$3.35 an hour, it'd take five four-hour shifts to net $55 after taxes. At that rate, I figured I could be in Guess jeans by the first night game of the Radnor High School football season. And I already had the socks.

'*Guess* what, Mom?' I said, maybe a little smugly, when I got home.

'What?'

'I applied for a job today.' I paused for dramatic effect. 'At The Limited. In the mall. So I don't need you anymore. I can get my own Guess jeans.' I was empowered.

She looked across the table, holding aces. 'How are you gonna get there?'

'Well, I'm gonna need a ride. Or I can just take the car. The open shifts are from four to eight, so you don't even use the car then anyway, and it's only three nights a week,' I said, trying to tone down the teen-power vibe.

'Kelly, if you think I am going to let you drive home from the King of Prussia mall at night, you've got another thing coming,' she said, as if I had asked to get my own apartment in West Philly. 'And I'm certainly not driving out there six times a week. End of conversation. And don't leave your book bag on the kitchen table.'

'That sucks,' I said, sort of under my breath as I pulled my bag off the table and headed toward the stairs.

'What did you say?' my mom said, burning a hole in my back with her stare. Although my brothers had thrown it out a few times, I had broken new personal ground with *sucks*.

I had a choice now, retreat with a 'nothing' or turn back and fight.

'I said, THAT SUCKS. That REALLY SUCKS.' I could have lifted a bus over my head, for all the adrenaline I had flowing. 'You say I can't have Guess jeans because they cost too much, so I go and get a job so I can pay for them myself and THEN you say, you can't have the job, you can't drive to the mall. I am SEVENTEEN years old, Mom. Denise Warner has been working three shifts a week at Thrift Drugs since she was a FRESHMAN.'

'Good for Denise Warner,' said my mom, never one for comparisons.

'Yeah! Good for Denise Warner is right! At least her mom is supportive and understands her and wants her to succeed in life!' I screamed, creating a causal relationship between success in life and Guess jeans. 'Why can't I drive to the mall? I've had my license for a year. Have I ever had an accident? A fender bender? A speeding ticket? NO. NEVER. But I might as well have run over an old lady — on my way home from a bar

— the way you act. Why don't you trust me?' I had elevated the argument from designer jeans to matters of trust and understanding. If I could get it to love, I could seal it.

'First of all, you better stop screaming this minute, missy. Second of all, I do trust you. I do not trust other people, however. I am not going to let my teenage daughter walk through a dark parking lot after the mall closes, get into a car alone, and drive down deserted roads. I don't care if you wanted to go feed the poor or join the Latin Club, it is not safe for you to drive a car, at night, alone. And that's final. Now get upstairs and stay there until I call you for dinner.'

I might have been softened by her single-minded devotion to my safety, but instead I stormed silently to my room, where I scratched out a long note in which the words 'I hate living in this house' and 'I wish Denise Warner's mom was my mom' punctuated a longer diatribe about the inhuman way I was being raised.

About a month later, just before the night football game, my mom said, 'So if you want, I'll take you out to King of Prussia today and if we find a pair of Guess jeans, you can try them on.'

'Seriously?' I asked in amped disbelief, as if she had handed me a brand-new Walkman II.

'Yes, but this is an early Christmas present,' she said, 'so just remember that when December twenty-fifth comes along and you don't have as much under the tree as your brothers.' I promised to remember. Of course I would remember. I'd probably be wearing them.

Georgia and I now do this same dance. I say 'No, no more candy, time to go. Put all your toys in the basket and go get your shoes' and then, if she does it all without too much trouble, when she gets into her car seat, I slip her a few more jelly beans. I giveth, I taketh away, and I concede the point, thirty years later, to my mother. And like my mother did that afternoon when I threw my arms around her in gratitude for the jeans, I accept Georgia's big, luscious thank-you begrudgingly, not sure who won that round or what lesson I just taught.

★ ★ ★

And now, the lamentable postscript to The Guess Jeans Fight of 1984.

From the perspective of a Catholic mother trying desperately to raise a nice Catholic girl who knew when to keep her legs closed (always), it can only be considered tragic to note the role those very pants played in the loss of my virginity.

I was a freshman at the University of Richmond and Jimmy Betts, a sophomore with hair as light and tousled as an angel's, was my first nonfictional boyfriend. He drove a white BMW and wore Duck Head khakis every day, until spring broke, and he switched over to cutoff Duck Head khakis. He had a couple of thick, colorful sweaters, like the ones Cliff Huxtable used to wear on *The Cosby Show*, and when he wasn't wearing them, I was. He said I had great legs, and nothing I had showed them off more than my Guess jeans. He was adorable, and he loved me the way only a nineteen-year-old can — suddenly and deliriously. Couplehood was all new to me, as was any contact with those pointy things that lived below the male belly button.

My mother had deterred my sexual awakening by trafficking in propaganda like, 'Your father certainly wouldn't have married me if I weren't pure.' The emphasis on *pure* was something akin to a code word used in an amateur sting operation. She found many ways to insinuate that any decent boy — a boy as good as my dad — wouldn't touch a girl who'd been touched already. And I bought it.

My mother's campaign was aided by my

own anxiety regarding the hairy, purple bundles I had accidentally seen once or twice, growing up with two brothers. I believe God may have fashioned the veiny penis and its revolting hanging bed pillow to dissuade women until their curiosity eclipses their aesthetic qualms. Or maybe, knowing that intercourse involved certain unsavory sights, smells, and sounds, God deliberately left the ingredients for alcohol lying around where man would undoubtedly find them.

Whoever gets the credit, I went off to college a virgin, which, once word got out, put a big round target on my crotch, a target that was eventually hit by Jimmy Betts, who convinced me over a hundred drunken nights that my mom wasn't talking about him, just the other guys. I was kind of tormented about it all, and I'm pretty sure Jimmy was in an exacting torment of his own. He slept in my bunk bed night after corked night for months while I snuggled him mercilessly. I wonder now how he made it all the way across campus every morning, if he was tempted to shine his sword (as my brothers would say) behind the power plant or even the nearest wide tree.

Eventually, my more experienced girl-friends got the best of me. Their campaign started with a genuine concern regarding my utter lack of gynecological attention to date. No one had ever suggested I see an ob-gyn, and somehow, in my Catholic estimation of things, being seen at the ob-gyn's office was effectively the same as being seen buying rubbers or getting an abortion. Over time, though, the pressure to have a Pap smear started to get to me, and I called my mom.

'So, Tracy and Missy can't believe I've never been to an ob-gyn.'

'Kelly,' my mom said glibly, 'you are an adult now. If you want to go to the touchy-feely doctor, that's your business.'

After boldly taking responsibility for my reproductive health, my roommates hosted a Q-and-A with me on intercourse basics. Over a six-pack of Milwaukee's Best and a pack of Merit Ultra Lights, I exposed my ludicrous naïveté with questions like, 'So, like, how many times do you go in and out?'

As final preparation for my passage into womanhood, I wrote a one-act play where a newly defiled girl confronts her mother, which my creative writing class actually performed. I named my character Meggie Contini, a subtle literary allusion to *The Thorn Birds*, a comparable epic that also challenged notions of Catholic morality.

A week later, in February of my freshman year, I wiggled out of my hard-won Guess jeans, lay back in a twin bed on a sagging mattress, and sweet Jimmy Betts put the whole drama behind me in less than two minutes. I was a woman now. I had, after terrific consternation, disobeyed the Catholic Church and Mary Corrigan.

That summer, my mom's friend Susan Scheeler called my mom to say she had found a condom in her daughter's beach bag. My mom just laughed and said, 'Oh, Susan, come on, if your daughter was still a virgin at her age, you'd wonder if she was a lesbian.' Susan Scheeler's daughter was about to start her senior year *in high school*.

All that crap about purity — ha! Clearly, it was time for me to grow up and take control.

15

'I'm okay. I can take care of things,' I promise as I send Edward to work. 'The girls are at Amie's until noon and I'm going to look at some of these books people sent. I'll be fine.'

Lance Armstrong, no. Homeopathetic pain management, no. Learning to live with cancer, no. Alone with my bald head and my tumor, I stare in the mirror for a while and then press my breast to feel the lump that I can now picture so clearly and wonder if the chemo is doing anything at all.

Needing a boost, I call Greenie's cell. 'Yeah, you've got George Corrigan's cell phone. You know the drill. Good luck to a grand guy or a grand gal.' Beep.

'Oh hey, it's me. Everything's fine — quiet. Feeling pretty good. Bald but good. I think I'm bored. Okay, talk to you later.'

Still needing a boost, I send out an e-mail, tinkering with every sentence. It has to be upbeat so people won't worry too much and funny so they won't be scared to write back.

121

It's a big job, being the first person your age to get cancer.

To: All
Date: September 13, 2004, 9:11 p.m.
Re: Latest News

Chemo, I must say, isn't that bad. A nurse named Catherine pushes a butterfly needle into my port (imagine a Frankenstein bolt near the collarbone) and I sit there for five hours talking with Edward and flipping through magazines and watching people knit. I usually doze off for some part of it (they have warm blankets for the patients). After three years of mothering, I find the quiet kind of heavenly.

As for my hair, I woke up on Friday with a hundred hairs on my pillow and over the course of the day, pulled more out by the handful. So with Georgia and Claire at my feet, we went out back and shaved my head. Edward assures me that my noggin is a wonder of symmetry and beauty but all the same, you might want to prepare your children.

And lastly, I've signed up for a medical marijuana trial, so if anyone cares to revisit their youth, grab your Pink Floyd albums, pack up some nachos, and head on over to

455 Mountain Avenue.

Thanks for all the hats. I wear them around the clock.

Love,
Kelly

I hit send and then sit there with my tea, waiting. After a few automatic replies from people who are out of the office or on vacation, I see e-mails from Allison Mundth, Emily Birenbaum, Booker, Tracy Tuttle. Within an hour, my in-box is fat with e-mails, which is exactly what I wanted.

In the middle of the list, I see something from my cousin Kathy. As I recall, we met in Ocean City, Maryland, when I was a kindergartner and she had just become a teenager. In an old Speedo and a blue bandana, she told a joke to a room full of boys, effortlessly putting every one of them under her spell. As if that wasn't enough, later that day, she pulled a dollar bill from her very own pink leather wallet in her very own denim purse to buy a black cherry Italian Water Ice from the ice cream truck. Naturally, I have revered her ever since.

Last summer, her twenty-year-old son was killed in a car crash. My dad called our house at seven in the morning, crying.

'Aw, Lovey,' he said in an unnaturally high

voice. 'Aw, Kel, Aaron Zentgraf died last night. Driving accident.'

'No, oh no.' Greenie and I cried together and Edward came up behind me and just held on until I hung up and rolled over. 'How will Kathy ever get out of bed?' I asked him. 'How will she ever stand up?'

Georgia was coming up on two and Claire was still just a newborn. Every time I looked at them that day, I cried.

★ ★ ★

It's been more than a year since Aaron died, and although I have left messages and sent e-mails, Kathy has stayed underground, which I can't begrudge her.

But there's her name, right there. In a couple unpunctuated lines, she says I am now one of them, 'the people who are aware of *other*.' She says Tony, her husband, thinks of it as a subculture.

So now I'm on the inside. Something about the way she phrases it makes me feel almost lucky, or maybe I am just pleased to be more like her, a person who has been made real, a person who has been sucked into a related, but separate, existence. At the same time, I feel like a deplorable phony whose pain couldn't possibly be in the same class as

Kathy and Tony's.

She also says, 'People think death is the worst thing that can happen but of course that's not true.' Impossible. I forward the e-mail to Edward with a string of question marks.

For weeks, Edward and I talk about it. What could be worse? We cheer the girls on as they come down the slide and watch them kiss themselves in the hall mirror and listen to them sing 'This Old Man' in the backseat. We say to each other, 'Nothing could be worse.' But then we hear about our old friend Luke whose twenty-year-old daughter weighs ninety pounds and hates the sight of herself. Luke, who is alone again after another awful divorce, is scared to go to work, terrified his daughter will kill herself by skipping her protein shake or running until she drops. My friend Josie is single and forty-six and born to be a mother, and nobody knows what to say to her as her ovaries dry up like raisins. She doesn't have half of what Kathy has. I mean, Kathy's pain exists because for twenty years, she loved her boy. Twenty years of love is a lot. It is more than all her suffering.

I get another e-mail from a particularly grown-up friend of mine, Jen Komosa. She just says, 'You are stronger than you think. You are strong *enough*.'

About seven years ago, her mom died from brain surgery complications, after two years of treatments, specialists, and paralysis. Jen knew, by the time her mom had been put in a wheelchair and was barely able to see or hear, that she wasn't getting better. Jen's mom was in her late fifties and had seen several of her many children married. She had burped her daughter's daughters and watched them chase fireflies and play house. But when Jen's sister called her at 3 A.M. one night to tell her that their mother had passed, Jen vomited on the floor next to her bed.

When I called Jen to check on her, she told me that people were swarming around doing what people do: flowers, food, cards, calls, favors. She said just about everyone said something like, 'Your mom had a good life. She had a lot of happiness. She was so uncomfortable. Now she's at peace.' Well, yeah, okay, good for your mom. But what about you? What about your peace? Your comfort? Who's gonna remember what you wore for Halloween that year or the name of your fifth grade teacher? Who's gonna loan you money to buy your first house or cry when your baby is born? Who's gonna sit in the front row of your play?

Look, Mom! This is the scene where we get engaged! Oh! You're gonna love this part!

Look at me in my white dress, Dad! How about this one — Edward and Dad play golf together! And in this next scene, we get pregnant! Hey look, Dad! Edward reads *Sports Illustrated* cover to cover JUSTLIKEYOU! Isn't this a good play? Don't you love it? Wait! There's more! Edward gets promoted in the third act! Don't go yet! Georgia is going to kindergarten next year! Wait 'til you see her first swim meet! Her tiger goggles! Please stay. We bought Claire tap shoes! This part coming up — ! Claire plays the harmonica! She's applying to Yale! Don't LEAVE — it gets so good!

16

Amelia Taylor was seven when her mom died. I met her shortly after that in her living room in Sydney, where I was interviewing to be her nanny.

How I came to be job hunting in Australia is beside the point, but I'll just say that GT coached lacrosse there a few years before, and the attention he got upon coming home was the modern-day equivalent of killing the fatted calf and feasting for days. He had hit the reset button and was now GT, *world traveler*. He had started playing the guitar, and his hair was all wiry and streaky because, as he explained in one of his many spellbinding stories, he'd let an Aussie girl put highlights in his bangs, presumably while he picked out notes on the hostel's loaner guitar.

I decided then that the whole point of leaving home is so you can come home again, new and improved. I wondered if some time abroad might not benefit my personal brand. I'd come back rolling my own cigarettes, drinking Steinlager, and proselytizing about recycling and American imperialism. I would be every annoying repatriated American, bent on enlightening her naive brethren.

So after saving for a year, I flew over to Australia with my college roommate, Tracy Tuttle. We spent the first couple months 'getting pissed at the pub,' making out with Europeans, and taking pictures of each other on beaches, and then it was time to find some paying work.

★ ★ ★

The Brown family had an indoor pool, and their children seemed easily entertained. I had just barely settled into my squalid au pair room when Mrs Brown asked me to join her in the living room 'to review everything.' 'Everything' turned out to be a lot different from what we talked about during the interview, before I unpacked my fifteen items of clothing and sent my parents a postcard with my new contact information and lots of exclamation points. 'Everything' included weekly chores like cleaning the pool tiles, vacuuming out both their cars, folding up newsletters for their small business (teaching chess strategies to devoted players around Sydney). I asked, like any self-respecting, formerly unionized American would, if these to-do items were in lieu of watching the kids or in addition to. This, apparently, was the wrong tack. It led me back to the living room a few days later 'just to check in,' during which Mrs Brown said she thought I wouldn't be a good fit for them. She said they were 'kind of experimenting' with an American but that they thought they might be better going back to Asians, who had 'worked out so well' over the years.

Emboldened by the fact that I would never see her again, and powered by my love of drama, I told her she ought to be ashamed of herself and slammed the door on my way out. I may have even screamed up to the kids, 'Hey, guys! Your mom just fired me because I won't scrub her pool tiles, so no movie tonight!' I spent the weekend calling up people from the help wanted ads, which landed me my second family, headed by a flight attendant named John who was newly widowed. I would be the first nanny since his wife died. Cancer. Her name was Peggy.

You could tell that the house had once been small, maybe a one bedroom, but over the years had sprawled out. A new kitchen, a couple of bedrooms, a pool, an in-law unit. There was no discernable style. Just lots of hand-me-downs from various uncoordinated sources.

Living in this crowded house were John, his two small children, Amelia and Martin, his twenty-one-year-old stepson, Evan, and his father-in-law, Poppa. It had been Peggy's house, bringing together her firstborn, her father, her husband, and her new children, under one roof, *her* roof. And then she got cancer and spent a lot of time 'in hospital' and they were all there, staring at one another, like what the hell are we all doing here?

I lived with them for four months, trying recipes she had marked as 'GOOD!' in her cookbooks, throwing away junk mail addressed to her, driving her pudgy, gorgeous, blue-eyed daughter to ballet, or taking a tongue-lashing from her four-year-old son for forgetting his sun hat, a required part of his school uniform. Every so often, I'd think, *They're okay, Peggy. It really seems like they're going to be okay.*

One night when John was at work getting cocktails for passengers on their way to Tokyo, I had an impromptu dinner with Poppa, Peggy's father. He poured some white wine, I made pasta with pink sauce, and we got to talking about his daughter.

'She came to get me after my wife died. She just said, 'Dad, we have room just for you in Sydney. We have a room with its own bathroom and a little fridge. We have an orange tree that needs help and you'll be in charge of laundry.' That's what she said.'

I smiled. My dad was famous for

constantly soliciting dirty clothes. I could hear him calling out, 'Lovey! I'm getting ready to do a load. Got anything for me?'

'When I got here, she had the place all set up for me. Even put the fridge on a card table so I didn't have to lean over. She thought she was going to take care of me . . . '

I nodded.

'Would you like some more?' he asked, lifting the wine bottle.

I nodded again. I had a nice buzz. The kids were back in their room doing a giant five-foot dinosaur floor puzzle. I could hear Amelia alternately cheering and berating her little brother. 'Good job, Martin! That's a good job!' and then without warning, 'No, Martin! Don't be dumb!'

'She was so healthy her whole life,' he said, looking straight into me, like maybe I could explain this to him. 'Never even broke her arm or had chicken pox . . . healthy like a horse . . . ' He looked down now, and conversation slowed.

'You must have been so shocked.' I urged him on. So much had been intimated over the months, but no one had ever really just sat me down and told me what happened to Peggy Taylor, what happened that required a twenty-four-year-old party girl to come shore up the family.

There was a long pause.

'I worry about the children. Amelia has been so mad. She switches her loyalties all the time — one day it's me, the next it's Evan, and when Martin comes home, she's all over him and grousing at the rest of us.'

'My brother GT would call that diversifying her risk.'

'Yep, that's it. She doesn't trust us.' He paused and then added, 'But she wants to.'

'She doesn't trust me either. She scolds me for putting too much Vegemite on her toast or forgetting her library books for school. She won't sit in my lap. She doesn't even like it when Martin sits in my lap. She wouldn't eat one of my cookies the other day.'

'Those were good cookies, dear.'

He usually called me Kelly.

'She's a special girl,' he said, as a fight broke out in the back bedroom. He started to take my plate and I stood up. 'I got it, Poppa. I got it. Can I bring you some tea, after I get those guys under control?'

He always made a cup of tea with lemon before he disappeared into his room for the night.

'No. Thanks, dear. Not tonight.' He stood up. I put my hand on his arm, touching him for the first time since we shook hands the day I moved in, and he leaned into me and kissed my forehead, making me blush.

He doddered off to his room, his face ruddy from the wine, and I headed back to the kids' room, warning them as I approached, 'Amelia! Martin! It's time to pick up. That's it for tonight, so let's — ' When I turned the corner I found them fighting over a book.

'It's not his!' Amelia pleaded. 'Mummy gave it to me! Kelly! Make him let go! Let go! Martin!'

I started in with the voice of authority — 'BOTH OF YOU! STOP!' — but when that failed to inspire even some passing eye contact, I started peeling Martin's fingers off the spine of an oversize, hardcover copy of *Where the Wild Things Are*.

'If you can't share it, you can't have it. But — ' They froze, in anticipation, listening for a way out. 'If you both clean up right this minute, I'll read it to you. But you have to clean up right this minute . . . '

So I read to them about Max, that cheeky boy who sailed in and out of days and over a year to a place where giant, clawed beasts gnashed and roared but Max, brave Max, just looked them right in the eye and said BE STILL and in so doing, came to rule them. For the kids' sake, I read the pages with great conviction, but I knew better.

17

There is fear, like the moment before a car accident or the jolt that shoots through you when you see your baby slip under water, and there is pain, like whacking your head into a cabinet door left open or the quiver in your shoulders as you carry your end of the sofa up those last few stairs, fingers slipping. And then there is pain and fear together, like delivering a baby or standing up for the first time after surgery. Until they tell you it's working, chemo is like that, pain and fear, fear and pain, alternating relentlessly.

Yesterday, I took eighteen pills in twenty-four hours for everything from the well-known side effects like nausea and fatigue to the secret ones like runaway infections and tearjerking constipation. Each side effect can be treated with medication, which usually has its own side effect. For nausea: Zofran. For the constipation caused by Zofran: laxatives and stool softeners. To ward off infection and stabilize your white blood cell count:

135

Neupogen. For the deep bone pain caused by Neupogen: Vicodin, which in turn causes nausea and drowsiness. And there you are, right back where you started.

I am glibly explaining all this to my mom when she tells me today is her birthday.

'Sixty-five today,' she says, with a remarkable lack of expectation or disappointment. Sixty-five and I didn't even come up with a card. She is forgiving, especially considering the hoopla I expect on my birthdays, even now that I am, as my family likes to joke, 'Edward's problem.' Somehow, I finished sewing that ottoman slipcover last week, and yesterday, I spent an hour at Old Navy loading up on more crap but didn't grab her a sweater or sew her a little pillow. But I am instantly exempted, like the slow kid who steals gum from the corner store.

I write a note to myself on the corner of a Kleenex box on my bedside table. 'MOM — 65!' Then I tell her I am going to church on Sunday with my friend Amie, who is a nice Catholic girl, because even though I'm not really going, this will make her happier than any present I could send.

As we are hanging up, Georgia tiptoes into my room, home from preschool, whispering about Gracie, who got in trouble for painting Morgan's legs, and hands me a little white bag.

'We went into the stooore and got your

136

druuuugs,' she says, all the while bringing her face closer and closer to mine until I nearly go cross-eyed trying to stare into those brown almonds. I sleep, off and on, all day and into the evening. Claire is sick and maybe teething, and she cries out after midnight. Normally, I am loath to lift her from the crib, believing that all the commotion will make it harder for her to get back to sleep, but when you are in pain, and you see someone else in pain, there is really nothing as satisfying as giving them comfort in the night. I hold her for a long time, in the dark, like sisters lost in a forest.

'It's okay, baby, I'm here. I know it hurts. I know. You're gonna be okay. Let's go back to sleep. It's okay. I'm here.'

I lay her down and tuck a white Egyptian cotton blanket around her funny little body. She sighs. One last shiver. A rustle. Silence. Oh God, look. I made someone all better.

I try to get back to sleep but am caught in the between place, gravity pulling my body into the mattress while my subconscious drags my mind from one thought to the next. I imagine that I am strapped to a conveyor belt, on my side, in my usual sleeping position. The belt chugs along against my will . . . first a shot, then an IV bag, then the pounding of the MRI machine, then breezes and a Corona, then Claire's warm body sleeping beside me, then a cold exam table at UCSF. A clipboard is propped up against me and a hundred little patient ID stickers are stuck to my face and arms. There are no levers on the machine, no way to control the speed, no stop button. I rest my eyes and let the belt take me where it will. Then I cup my hands around the belt to stop it, but I let go, afraid my skin will tear open and the blood won't clot ever again. Finally, finally, the second Vicodin takes over and it all goes to black.

The morning is horrible, hallmarked by bone pain and nausea and a headache. I cry to Edward about West Nile virus, which has reached Piedmont, the small town where we live. It killed a squirrel last week, and we all got warning pamphlets about standing water and other draws for mosquitoes. I cry like a kid who missed her nap, weary and weak and self-pitying.

'Am I gonna end up in the ER over a mosquito bite? Do I have more white blood cells than a squirrel?'

'You're almost done, Kel. One more to go. Come Christmas, you'll be completely finished with chemo. And in the meantime, let me clean up around the carport. There's water there we can get rid of, and we can spray outside and I can e-mail Suzie Eder at UCSF. We'll keep you safe, baby,' he says, as protective and kind as a father.

18

After a year on foreign soils, there were only five miles between me and Wooded Lane. Five miles, half a Twix, and the last cigarette. Driving with the sun behind me, I was bursting with tales — parasailing in southern Thailand, bungee jumping in New Zealand, trying space cookies in Fiji and kangaroo meat in Australia — one g'day after another, bush walks, barbies, bugger all, no worries, mate.

I beeped pulling into the driveway, and my mom came out to meet me. We had a quick hug, and then I lifted my rotting green backpack over my shoulder for the last time and followed her inside. She emphasized that they were having a Christmas party the next night, so would I please, 'for God's sake,' wait to unpack 'that thing' until after they 'got through' with that? Right then, I was annoyed. Already. But I refocused and said, 'That's fine, Mom, let's sit down. Let's get caught up. Did anyone call? Is there any mail for me? Is Dad home? Is GT coming over tonight? Who's coming to the party?' My mom spelled out her vision for the party

— bartender in the living room, self-serve in the den, and my friends were not, well, welcome. I was annoyed again. 'If you have a bunch of friends here,' she rationalized, 'you'll spend all night talking to them. I need you to help pass hors d'oeuvres and keep the place clean, and,' — she added, disingenuously — 'my friends are dying to hear about your trip.' That sounded fun, passing my mom's pigs in a blanket and telling Mr. Hodges about the hostels in Fiji while he sucked back his Christmas scotch.

I started to dig around in my backpack, looking for photographs to show her. 'This is Mike.' I pointed out a shaggy brunet in sunglasses. He was holding a beer with one hand and me with the other. 'He's from outside London. He was with us for a couple weeks in Australia and then was supposed to meet us in New Zealand. I'm surprised I haven't got a letter from him here. He has this address . . . ' He had probably written and she had misplaced it somewhere, what with all the preparations for the party.

I was practically breathless, bragging like you can pretty much only do to your parents. 'Oh — and this is the ninety-nine-foot dive boat we were on for five nights.' I pushed a couple pictures across the table. 'We even did a dive at night — to see the fish that only come out in the dark.' My mom was not adventurous and did not easily part with a dollar. Paying good money to swim around in cold, black water with a flashlight probably sounded like the idiotic decision of a self-indulgent child.

Next I tired her with a glowing description of Cape Tribulation, in the northeast — the Maine of Australia. Like Maine, it's a magnificent setting where fortunate people go to ooh and ahh and generally eschew the big-city rat race. I showed her a picture of me, bloated from months of sausage and beer, in nothing but a bathing suit riding a horse bareback on the beach, the rain forest to my left and the barrier reef to my right.

In midstory about how, one night, I sang *onstage* with a band in Cape Trib, I told her to hold on while I went to the bathroom. When I came back, there was a shady snapshot on the table of my mom standing next to my dad, who was in a hospital bed, surrounded by flowers. Apparently, it was taken on my dad's last birthday, which, as my mom then explained, he spent recovering from surgery.

'What kind of surgery?' I asked, still standing, still staring into the photograph.

'Your father had cancer,' she said as her voice started to crack.

So, while I was nannying in Sydney, making Vegemite sandwiches, and learning to drive a minivan on the other side of the road, my dad was diagnosed with the very thing that killed his father: prostate cancer. My mom told me about his sky-high PSA count, long, confusing meetings with surgeons and oncologists, agreeing to surgery over radiation, manning the phones, checking him into the hospital.

'I'll let your dad tell you the whole story, but all his brothers — Dickie, Gene, Jimmy — had it. They all had surgery — every one of them — in April.'

'Wait — what? Seriously? They all had cancer? Isn't that what Pop had? They all had surgery?'

I can only imagine the stir this created in Catholic churches, flower shops, and golf clubs along the I-95 corridor. Dickie in Boston, George in Philadelphia, Gene in Greensboro, and Jimmy in Winston-Salem. My mom said the brothers talked on the phone constantly, comparing notes on everything from ice chips and pudding to visiting hours and nurses. Not one of them even considered getting a second opinion; they trusted one another.

My dad had his prostate removed. During the operation, a tiny blade accidentally nicked my dad's bladder. His recovery was long and complicated. Some people told him he should sue, but he always shook his head and said, 'I'm not the suing kinda guy.'

The problems after his surgery were serious; a catheter for thirty days, recurring fevers. One afternoon, my mom said with a shaky voice, he collapsed in the laundry room. She cried when she told me about calling an ambulance. She said she had never known fear like that. My dad was a terrible patient, frustratingly optimistic. She said ten minutes before he collapsed with a 105-degree fever, he called from the road to see if she needed anything from the grocery store. Her eyes were red and puffy now. She said she couldn't trust him to tell her how he was feeling, to pick up his prescriptions on time, to drink enough water, to rest. Then she got herself together and wrapped it all up in a sentence or two. It's all over now, and he's as good as new.

The phone rang. She'd generally let the queen of England leave a message, but that day, she welcomed the interruption. She was done with the cancer talk.

'Hello?' she said, taking a restorative breath.

I sat stupidly at the table, looking at my pictures next to hers.

* * *

I called GT that night. 'So I just have to say — it blows my mind that no one thought I should know that Dad had cancer. It just blows my mind that you would — that you could — that he would go to surgery and no one would tell me. I mean, what if he — God forbid — what if he died on the table? God forbid. How would you have explained it to me? Who decided that I couldn't — that I was such a child — that I couldn't be included? Am I ever going to be considered an adult? Are you still going to protect me when I'm forty? Fifty? Were there decisions to be made? Did he have choices? You know some people — like Missy's dad — choose not to have their prostrates removed at all.'

'Prostate, Kelly. Prostate. There's no r,' he said.

'Yeah, okay, prosTATE. So can you please tell me what happened?'

He sounded so expert. He said everyone agreed there was no sense in telling me and ruining my trip. No one wanted me to come home early or be calling all the time — overemotional, a drain in an already draining time. He was so sure of himself, so fluent with the terms, the rationale for each decision, the side effects and ongoing risks.

144

Here I was, trying to be more like GT, adventurous, globe-trotting GT, and he had moved on. He had met the doctors and been in the waiting room. He had sat with my dad in his hospital room and managed outbound communications with aplomb. He had been useful, a good child, while I had been badgering my mom to renew my driver's license for me since I forgot to go to the DMV before I left.

Later, I looked through all the letters they had written to me. They wrote about my mom winning her bridge tournament and how Booker had started coaching lacrosse in Baltimore. GT had a band now. I tried to remember our overseas calls. I remember telling them about how kangaroos lay around golf courses, common as rabbits, about seeing God-spell at the Sydney Opera House, about waitressing at The Fishbone Grille in New Zealand.

I asked my dad to explain all this to me, but he came back with his usual broad-stroke optimism. 'Lovey, we got it done!'

'Well, are you okay now? Is it totally better? Could it come back?'

'Naw, nothing's coming back, Lovey. There's nowhere for it to come back to, you know what I mean?' he said, laughing and patting my leg. 'No prostate, no cancer, no worrying, right, Lovey?'

'Greenie,' I said, feeling fragile, 'I'm sorry I wasn't here to help you. Or just to keep you company.'

'Aw, Lovey, I was in good hands. Your mother's a force — Florence Nightingale! She had it under control.'

'She just never let on. It's incredible,' I said.

I learned, in time, how parents instinctively occupy their children with petty chatter or new dolls while the fights, the crying, the peril of life swirls mercifully over their heads. I also learned that preserving your children's untroubled state is vital. It is the thing that you say to yourself late in the night, the thing that finally lets you fall asleep. At least, you say, the kids are okay.

$$\star \quad \star \quad \star$$

The day after the Christmas party, my mom set up 'The Store,' her annual processing of the unnecessary gifts she had received over the year from friends thanking her for dropping them at the airport or watching their house while they were in Florida. A platter here, a set of matching coffee mugs there. Some items appeared in their original wrapping paper, as if they'd never been opened. She could open them so carefully that after she surveyed the contents, she'd just wrap them back up and press the tape right back into place. Then, in pencil, she'd write lightly on the bottom 'zebra frame' or 'bath salts.'

Inventory bulked up around her birthday, an event that drew the same line each year: 'Please, no gifts. Just a few kind words.' More items came in over the summer, when houseguests came through Wooded Lane more frequently. My mother was rarely anyone's houseguest herself; the prospect of being indebted to anyone made her face screw up as if she had gone to the garage and found the trash cans knocked over. And she probably assumed that others felt as she did about the matter: hosting was an odious business, akin to the insufferable office Christmas party.

Before The Store opened, you could hear her in there moving things around and humming. It made her happy — her product line, her well-timed service, her neat solution to the nuisance of hostess gifts. When the door opened, the twin beds were covered with ten, maybe fifteen, small gifts that were just right for an aunt we hadn't seen in a while or Marty, the short-order cook down at Joe's Place where we went for eggs after church, or really any of the people we had likely overlooked in our holiday shopping. Scraps of yellow legal pad paper sat on or beside each item with the price written in blue ballpoint pen. She made a big deal out of not charging tax and seemed to emphasize it with a dash, as in, $6 — . Cash was exchanged, since, 'What kind of people would we be if we didn't pay for the presents we gave?'

A silk scarf would have cost $12, making it the most expensive item on the bed; my mom would've suggested it for GT's godmother, Peggy. GT would've bought that with a wad of one-dollar bills. Under pressure, GT was an easy marble to roll, something my mother and I both knew, and there was something about him, even then, that gave you the feeling that he could afford it. Maybe it was because he scored big on the SATs. Or it could've been his businessman hairdo, I can't say for sure.

As my mom described the features and benefits of the scarf, she'd assure GT that he could give it to Peggy with confidence. By this, my mom meant that the person who had given her the scarf would not be in the room. This guarantee came with every item and was essential to the success of the venture. Regifting was a dicey business, although you'd have never known it from watching my mom nod proudly as we passed off her unwanted things to our aunts and uncles.

I can't hold it against her any longer, since not only did I avail myself of her timely service many times, but just last week, I smiled graciously as I gave my good friend Shannon some expensive decorative candles in a very classy gift bag. Both the candles and the bag were given to me by my good friend Chad, who I like to imagine had received them from yet a third person. 'The Store' goes down in family history as 'fraud lite.' But I knew by the way my mom smiled as GT gave Peggy the scarf that she had a comfort with and a skill for recasting things to her liking and, moreover, that she had her own rubric for what was 'a lie' and what was 'none of your business.'

19

So my mom calls tonight and mentions that my dad had some blood in his urine last week, and that he ran into Dave Ellis at a lacrosse game and Dave Ellis is some kind of urologist at the local hospital and Dave told him to come on in and he'd take a look and so, my mom says, sounding exasperated, like Dave Ellis is some bastard stirring up all this trouble, it turns out it's cancer and well, you know, he had something like this last year and they didn't mention it to me because what could I do and I start crying and Edward's dad is in the kitchen because tomorrow is Thanksgiving and he is cooking for us because I just had my seventh round of chemo and he hears all this and he fixes me a drink and I am THISfuckingCLOSE to throwing the drink against the living room wall, storming straight out the front door, slamming it until it splinters, putting the phone under my car wheel, and driving back and forth and back and forth until it is crushed, all the while screaming and honking and pissing my pants and pounding the wheel until someone gets a long needle and a straitjacket and promises a hundred times that nothing and nobody is going to take my father away from me.

PART TWO

A father is always making his baby
into a little woman.
And when she is a woman
he turns her back again.

~ ENID BAGNOLD

20

I had never missed a Christmas on Wooded Lane, so it was understandable that my parents objected when I announced that, single and twenty-nine, I was spending the six weeks from Thanksgiving through New Year's hiking in Nepal.

'Nepal?' my mom said, like I was headed to Uranus with nothing but my cashed-out 401(k).

'Yes, *Nepal*,' I mimicked, 'where Mount Everest is.'

'Well, I certainly hope you aren't going to climb it,' she said, implying that a current passport and some sturdy boots were the only requirements for summiting Everest.

The next day, my mom called. 'You know, Kelly, I was at Betty Moran's last night and half the people there didn't even know where Nepal is.'

'It's right between India and China,' I said.

'Yes, I know. I looked it up in my atlas,' she said. Going to Nepal, it seemed, was right below getting a tattoo and voting for Dukakis on the 'Ten Best Ways to Crap on Your Parents' list. I went anyway, even though I felt funny about missing the routine — the

155

shrimp cocktail platter that Booker and GT pick at before it's even out of the fridge, the fight over what time to leave for Baltimore, the last-minute negotiations around regifting. I went because a guy named Bob Burch, who had traveled almost everywhere, told me that Nepal was the best place he'd ever been. I went because I was still single and wanted to avoid another set of dateless holidays. And I went because a girl I knew came home from Nepal fifteen pounds thinner. (Apparently, 'it just fell off.')

Nepal, about the same size as Arkansas but with ten times the people, started for me in Kathmandu, with the bikes, dogs, potters, and weavers, the locals selling rugs, spices, brass Buddhas, and tiny transistor radios so you could tune into one of the seven or eight stations in the country. Everyone seemed to be wearing a sweater made of the same four yarns — brown, gray, purple, and magenta. The only other color in the palette was saffron, which the monks wore.

After a few errands — trading traveler's checks for rupees, getting a trekking permit, renting a down jacket and sleeping bag — I took a local bus to the bottom of the trail. I felt very brave. The woman seated next to me had an upside-down live chicken in each hand.

'Namaste,' she said.

'Namaste,' I repeated.

After a couple hours, the bus let me off on the side of a road and someone pointed to a trail barely wide enough for a golf cart. There was no sign. While the bus pulled away, I just stood there, awaiting some sort of confirmation. As I was pulling my map out of my pack, two fast-talking, skinny-legged German guys hopped out of a car and bounded past me without a second's pause.

'Bhulbule?' I called after them, naming the first village on the map.

'Yaa, yaa, Bhulbule!' one called back, without stopping. I think the other one was lighting a joint. They were practically skipping.

Four hours later — four hours of walking along a trail that often felt too narrow and faint to possibly be right, four hours without seeing any other trekkers, four hours of alternating between pride and regret — I came up a hill and saw three huts in a clearing. To my left was a patch of flat land where a hunched man walked beside a mule that was dragging a hoe about the size of two hands in the shape of a V. To my right was a woman in flip-flops and a sari with a basket of wood on her head as big as an ottoman. Ahead was a little house with prayer flags flying from poles on every corner, and on the side, someone had painted BHULBULE GUEST HOUSE.

So this is how it's gonna be, I thought.

'Namaste,' I said, pulling out my rupees for a lovely woman about my age who then walked me to a small room.

As she left, I lay back onto a low bed and stared at the wall across from me, which was made of large whitewashed rocks laid like bricks, and at my backpack leaning against it, which was made of aluminum, molded foam layers, and ripstop nylon. After a while, I pulled out my journal and a pen and found a sunny spot on a bench outside where I could watch the man work his field. I wondered how it was possible that tomorrow morning, his American counterpoint would climb up into a John Deere tractor, and without setting his foot on soil or breaking a sweat, till a field ten times as big, all the while listening on his headphones to Howard Stern talk about lesbian strippers with Robin.

Other trekkers were also outside in the last of the day's sun. The woman in charge was shuffling around with pillows and metal trays. Kids were playing with a wooden recorder and crawling around in the dirt. I looked around at the brown hills and behind them, the snowy mountains, and wondered if any of these children would ever see an ocean.

Could they even imagine it? What would they make of the Las Vegas strip or a data server center? For that matter, would I ever be able to describe Nepal to my parents? Maybe that's what happens, you go places and do things that are beyond your parents' capacity to imagine or understand, and that's how you start thinking of them as quaint and peripheral.

On the trail, no matter what time you arrived, dinner was served at seven. Wood was hard to come by, so the cook waited until everyone was in for the night to boil water and heat dal bhat, which was vegetables and lentils in gravy. We'd all sit around a single table on benches with our legs in the middle. Under the table, dug down into the dirt, was a low flat tray of embers. Strips of blanket nailed around the edge of the table kept the heat trapped and the visitors close. After dinner, someone — sometimes a sherpa, sometimes a trekker — would pass around a little pipe and we'd talk politics or the environment or consumerism over thin tea served in dented metal cups. The pot, the views, and the accents worked on me such that a few weeks into it, I was open to anything.

About halfway around the Annapurna trail, I sat down for breakfast next to a sunny German woman named Sabine and her three-year-old, Peter. While her son played with his soft-boiled egg and she nudged him along in German, Sabine explained that this was her third trip to Nepal. She usually stayed in Kathmandu, where she studied Buddhism, but this time, she was enjoying showing her son the Himalayas.

'I don't actually know much about Buddhism,' I admitted, smiling at Peter. 'I just know there are four truths, right?'

The first one, Sabine said, was that suffering was inevitable for all of us since, ultimately, any happiness you might feel will not hold against the certain onset of age, illness, or death. That seemed right, even though, at twenty-nine, I was unacquainted with age, illness, and death.

The second truth was that suffering was caused by craving pleasure and avoiding what is unpleasant.

'Yeah, I see that,' I said. 'So, what do you do? Not crave pleasure or pleasant things?'

'Well, sort of. That's the third truth: suffering will only end when you eliminate your desires. In other words, when you break your attachments.'

After eight years living off a United Way salary, I assured her, my attachments were minimal.

Sabine smiled, in a sweetly condescending way, and said, 'Not just material attachments.

All attachments — attachments to ideas, to goals, to jobs, to people.'

'People?'

'Yes, even people.'

I was proud of my attachments to people — my parents, Tracy Tuttle, Booker and GT. I mean, sure, don't attach to marble counter-tops or the Burberry fall line. But people? I say attach, wrap around, braid yourself into. What's the point of a life without attachments? We *are* our attachments.

'I don't get that. Like, take my dad. Am I not supposed to be attached to my dad?'

'Attachment turns the wheel of suffering. You can't hope to avoid suffering if you refuse to give up your attachments.'

'Oh.'

Then I'll suffer, I thought. *Then I choose suffering.*

The Catholics seemed to imply that it was safe to attach, since we'd all be reunited in heaven, but that had always felt too good to be true.

The fourth truth about the Eightfold Path was more than I could fit in my head and the sun was getting higher. I was ready to walk again. I liked Sabine — her voice, her deep dimples, the way she talked to her son. But she was lying if she thought she wasn't attached to that boy of hers, who made her eyes flicker every time he leaned into her.

On the trail that day, which was a climb of a thousand small steps made of rocks jammed into the hillside, I learned to keep my head down and keep moving. Stopping, looking up, calculating how much more was ahead — these were counterproductive. I moved slowly, but I moved. At a turn, I noticed a sherpa and his patron far below me. Within an hour or so, they were at my back.

'Hello there,' a cheery Brit said. This was Paul, who, I learned on the climb, was an accountant for the BBC in London. He had more breath than I did, and so did most of the talking. He had been everywhere — underground caving in Turkey, scuba diving in the Red Sea, whale watching in New Zealand. He said he took a couple months off every year from work because 'How seriously can I take myself? I'm just one of six billion people, right?'

The world's population was something I knew but hadn't considered. I tried hard to imagine six billion of anything — leaves, nuts, pebbles. If six billion grains of salt were one deep on a kitchen floor, how big would that kitchen floor be? And then how meaningless would it be to take one grain away? How unactualized would you be if you obsessed over one single grain?

21

My dad has cancer. Again. It's been confirmed now by several Main Line doctors. I've been online for days, at the oddly named Bladder Cancer Web Cafe, where I spend surreal moments leaning closer and closer to my computer screen, staring into photographs of bladder tumors that are as beautiful and disgusting as jellyfish. On a statistics page, I notice that about 40,000 men get bladder cancer every year, which turns out to be about the same number of women who die every year from breast cancer. I have often misquoted numbers by an order of magnitude, but 40,000 always sticks. Sometimes it seems breathtaking and other times, like when the host of the Oscars says hello to the 'billion people watching tonight!' or 95,000 kids are orphaned in a genocide, 40,000 dead women hardly seems worth all the pink fuss.

But today, I am just worried about one person, one old guy who, truth be told, has had more good years than most. Because I want more of him. Because I'm greedy.

The bladder cancer site reminds me of the first few days after I was diagnosed. My mother knew the woman who created breastcancer.org, so I started there. Twenty links and fifteen minutes later, I was filling out an online form that would calculate my odds. My age, the size of my tumor, the grade of my cancer. That's how I learned that at thirty-six, there was a 38 percent chance I'd be dead in five years.

I don't know what I'll find now as I click on 'Bladder Cancer Staging' and 'Invasive Transitional Tumors,' but I'm in a hurry to find it. It's like I'm driving and I'm lost but instead of slowing down, I am gunning it — hunched over the wheel, squinting at street signs, turning impulsively. And then in the headlights I see this: 'After bladder cancer invades the muscular layers of the bladder wall it may spread to bone, liver, and lungs.' I let go of the mouse and lean back in my chair. So that's what we need to know: is it invasive?

I call home, but the machine picks up. My mom's recorded message is brief and matter-of-fact followed by ten seconds of dead air before the beep.

'Hey, it's me. Give me a call, please,' I say, like I'm their mother and they've been ignoring me.

On a British site, I find a medical

illustration of the bladder area, which I print out to study. The kidneys, like two giant mushrooms, are nestled right behind the lowest ribs. Hanging off the kidneys are two tubes — the ureters — that appear to be about five inches long and lead to the bladder, which is like a fist.

I keep clicking to find the names and numbers of the national experts. I am looking for a hero. Here's one: Mark Schoenberg. He wrote the book on bladder cancer, literally, the one that popped up when I searched on Amazon. He works ninety minutes from Wooded Lane at Johns Hopkins. I call home again, and this time, Greenie picks up.

'Yes, sir!' he says.

'Hey, so I found the guy. He's at Hopkins. His name is Mark Schoenberg. I have the main number here; do you have a pen?' I say before my dad says a word.

'We'll figure it out, Lovey. We'll get it going,' my dad says.

Why can't he just do what I say? Why can't he stay on point?

'Do you have a pen?' I ask.

'Lemme tell you what I'm doing tomorrow. I'm gonna head over to Ellis's office and talk to the gal there. She's gotta sign an insurance form or something,' he says.

Right at this moment, this insufferable

moment, I hate him. He is irritating and foolhardy, like the star of the high school basketball team who skips the SATs since, ten to one, he's gonna go pro.

'Let's talk about forms in a second, Dad. Here's the main thing — ' I pause. I have to get this one thing through to him. 'In my opinion, it doesn't matter which doctor you *like*, all that matters is which doctor is the *best*, which doctor has seen the most cases, has access to the most current research, has the best machines and scanners and probes.'

He seems to be listening. Or maybe he's watching the day's sports scores on ESPN.

'This Hopkins guy,' I say, 'Schoenberg. He's THE guy. He wrote the book I sent you. He's probably the number one guy in the country, which might make him the number one guy in the world, and he's in your backyard.'

I think I'm getting through.

'Now, we gotta get him to see you. And fast,' I say, believing that somehow we'd be able to get Greenie an appointment. 'Assuming we can find a way in, Hopkins will want your biopsy report.'

'Oh, I gotta get that,' he says like he forgot mayonnaise at the grocery store. 'I'll ask that gal for it tomorrow. You know, I left her a message — '

'Tell her you have to have it today. Don't let her run you around. It's your information and you need to be your own advocate,' I say, using the very same terms that were used with me. 'You could have her send it directly to Schoenberg, but with *my* films, we took them to UCSF ourselves, to be sure.'

'We'll get it done.'

'So, have you talked about whether it's invasive?' I ask, jumping to my next agenda item.

'Jammy — ' I hear my dad call up to my mom, using her grandmother name.

'What?' My mom picks up upstairs, talking too loud.

'Kelly wants to know if it's invasive,' my dad says, sounding apologetic because maybe she was having a rest or touching up her fingernail polish.

'I don't know if it's invasive, Kelly. I don't think he said,' my mom says.

In the past, I have been accused of treating my mother like a ninny, like when she tells a waiter she'll have the saLmon, not only pronouncing the *L* but emphasizing it, like she knows something the rest of us don't. So I stifle the need to scream at her: 'YOU DON'T KNOW IF IT'S INVASIVE? That's THE question!' I want to, though, and so later that night, when Edward asks me how

167

they're doing, I scream, 'THEY DON'T EVEN KNOW IF IT'S INVASIVE!'

'Lovey,' says my dad, wrapping up the call, 'we're in good hands. I can tell you that.' I can hear his patent faith coming through, which is fine and nice and good for him but look at all the faithful starving and rotting on their way to and from church. 'We'll talk to you in a little bit. We're headed to noon mass. We'll call you back.'

He always says this, that he'll call me back, even at the end of long conversations when we've exhausted every imaginable topic. 'Lovey, lemme call you back — ' he says, like he can't get me off the phone.

I am at odds with everyone, and it's making me lonely. My most special person is dying, and no one is doing anything right. My mom, I'm almost sure, is playing dumb. Or maybe she's decided to cup her ears and sing the ABCs until people stop saying awful things she doesn't want to hear. Booker infuriates me by resigning immediately.

'You know, Kel, if this is it, he's had a great life,' he says as I sob into the phone.

'What are you talking about?' I say with disgust.

'I'm just saying, we all gotta go sometime and he'll never look back and think he should have done things differently.' *No shit*, I think.

So does that mean we shouldn't bother getting a second opinion?

'Yeah, well, um, okay,' I say, like we have nothing more to talk about. 'I gotta go. I gotta call GT.'

'Kelly — ' he says in the tone people use with me when they think I am overreacting. People like Booker, GT, Edward.

'No, don't worry about it. I'll call you tomorrow when I know more.'

Within the first minute of my call with GT, it's clear we both assume we'll be the main point of contact for the doctors.

'Why don't I give Dave Ellis a call?' GT says.

'Well, do you even know what to ask him? Have you been online? Because I have. And I have a list of questions here.'

'I don't think we want to alienate Dr. Ellis with a bunch of questions. Let me call him.' Then GT plays the lacrosse card. 'Ellis is a lacrosse fanatic. He'll talk to me.'

'This is a fa-tal di-sease, GT. We're not trying to get into a fucking golf club,' I say through set teeth. Then, in the new silence, I play my card. 'You don't know the vocabulary. You don't know the questions — tumor grade, staging, node involvement.'

'Now wait. I can't remember . . . which med school did you go to? Was it Yale? Stanford?'

'Very funny,' I say as if I don't think

169

anything is funny anymore.

'Hey, you know Schoenberg? It turns out Dad coached a guy he works with, Jerry Schnydman, over in England, in like 1954.'

'Really?' I should have known this would be solved as all things in our family always had been — through relationships, most of which were born on a lacrosse field. 'Have you called him?'

'He said he'd call Schoenberg and call me back in fifteen minutes.'

'This is huge. Oh God, GT. Thank you.'

We agree to talk later. On the way to the bathroom, I lean into the hall mirror and shake my head, noting that my last few eyelashes are gone. My eyebrows fell out a month ago. My whole head, including my face, is bare and smooth, like a salamander's.

★ ★ ★

Christmas, oblivious to our circumstances, comes anyway. My brothers and I are celebrating in California while my parents are at home, bracing themselves for Greenie's first chemo. I'm mad at my mother and then I'm mad at myself for being mad at my mother. Greenie would be here, but she is exhausted and scared and sick of flying to California.

Edward empathizes with my mother, which I try not to let shame or annoy me.

'Well, Kel, I gotta say, at least your mom is trying to take care of herself. She's been taking care of a lot of people lately. This is the first time in five months that she has put herself first, and you know, she's not even doing that. She's really putting your dad first.'

'But he wants to be here!' I say, trying to decide if I am fighting the good fight or just being a brat who wants a pony for Christmas even though I'm old enough to know that we can't afford one.

'Yeah, I know, but he should probably rest up,' Edward says, like he's never seen a Hollywood movie and doesn't know what the right ending is.

I know my dad doesn't really believe in rest, which is probably a factor in my mom's decision. I know that Christmas in California with grandchildren jumping on him, begging him to go to the park or read another book or take them to the movies is not a good idea. *I know*. But we're talking about a man who played pond hockey with high school kids when he was seventy-two. He even bought himself a new hockey stick at Wayne Sporting Goods for the occasion. My mom came home from a bridge game to the smell of melting fiberglass; my dad was curving his blade over

171

the stove before he met the guys out at the pond, 'just for a few minutes, Mare, I promise.'

My mom won't budge. I promise to stop asking. 'Thank you,' she says. 'You know, we don't even know when your father will start chemo. He could get a call from the doctors any minute now.'

'Okay, Mom. But let me just say one thing. What if this is — ' I still can't figure out if she knows what's happening but if she doesn't, it's probably not my place to tell her. 'Whatever. You gotta do what you gotta do. I know you're tired.'

★ ★ ★

The next night, Edward and I are due to take my brothers over to my friend Chad's cocktail party. The babysitter is divvying up tortellini for the girls as the rest of us scramble to get ready. Booker wears cords with a cotton sweater, since he is allergic to wool. He is lacing up boots that we used to call 'shit kickers' because for parties, he leaves his Nikes at home. GT wears something striking and expensive from a bitchy but stylish old girlfriend. I'm wearing a trendy, forgiving tunic with black pants and a cheery new hat I got just for this party. Where usually my brothers would have teased me that I looked like Debbie Gibson, tonight they say they like my 'groovy lid.' Compliments don't move easily among us.

We settle into the party and I love it that they are here and that we're back to doing what we always do — talking too loud, drinking too fast, holding on to one another. I get Booker going on some of his best teaching stories, because I want my new friends to know that Booker is the special teacher who students never forget. I want them to know that Booker sends every kid in his class a handwritten letter over the course of the year, telling him that he noticed that good thing they did, that he can see great things ahead. I look over at GT, who is winding up, getting ready to tell one of his epic tales. When he's ready, the room will be his. For the moment, he offers to get a woman another glass of wine, even though he doesn't know which way the kitchen is.

People are streaming in without knocking. Everyone's up. Then the doorbell rings, so I lean around the corner to wave in whoever it is and there, on the front step, are my parents — my mom, in her sequined Christmas wreath sweater from the golden age of shoulder pads and Ronald Reagan, and Greenie, in his UNICEF Santa Claus tie

— singing 'Joy to the World.' As everyone screams and yells and hugs, my mom keeps laughing and wiping away tears and pointing at me, saying, 'I GOT YOU! I GOT YOU!'

'When did you do this?' everyone wants to know.

'Mom! Mom! Oh my God!' I say, over and over again.

Apparently, she says, Greenie was moping around for days until finally, just yesterday, she said, 'Is there anything I can do to make this a merry Christmas?'

'Take me to California.'

'Go ahead,' she said. 'Call the airlines.'

The party goes on, and at some point, my mom comes and puts her arm around my waist and squeezes me into her and says quietly without looking at me, 'I did this for you, Kelly.'

She was positively lit up.

'I can't believe it, Mom. I can't believe you came. Thank you so much,' I say, shaking my head and leaning into her, wanting to give her whatever she wants for this, whatever praise, applause, recognition, whatever will bring out her lionheart again.

22

If you want to feel good or you need twenty bucks, talk to my dad. If you want to solve a problem, you might do better with someone else. If you're on the only important business trip you've ever had and you have a panic attack, keep looking until you find my mom.

It was 1999 and everyone in San Francisco was walking around thinking they might start the next Priceline or iVillage or Netscape. Some company called theglobe.com shot up 900 percent on its first day of trading and made instant millionaires out of everyone on the payroll, even though right there on the first page of the paperwork it said, plain as wall-to-wall carpet: 'The company expects to incur losses for the foreseeable future.' But that's the snotty voice of hindsight. At the time, I was thirty and right in there with the rest of the kids at the big Easter egg hunt, running in manic circles looking for gold in the grass.

My big idea was to develop a line of educational software to help high school English students learn the classics and in so doing, make CliffsNotes seem as outdated as

Wallabees and cowl necks. I went to sleep most nights imagining fawning profiles in *BusinessWeek* or *Wired* with a David and Goliath slant, something like 'Twentysomething Throws Notes off Cliff.' I asked GT and my mom to invest $20,000 each, which they did with the understanding that I would find a better name for the company than Shamrock Studios, because my mom said, 'the Irish aren't famous for their business sense; they're more into manual labor, like Shamrock Movers.' Thus was born Stratford Studios, a reference to Shakespeare's hometown.

Within a month, a prominent San Francisco law firm with assistants in Ann Taylor suits incorporated Stratford Studios in Delaware because Delaware offered certain tax benefits for C Corporations. The reason I became a C Corp, instead of something more appropriate like a sole proprietor, was so that I could issue stock options to employees. That I had no employees was no matter. I was poised to explode onto the NASDAQ. Legally, at least.

I made the first CD-ROM with two friends who signed excessive paperwork over cheap red wine at the plywood desk in my apartment — an NDA (nondisclosure agreement) to protect the confidentiality of our top secret work, the assignation of intellectual property rights, etc. We toasted to hard work, creativity, and my two investors, one of whom kept asking when our CD-RON would be ready.

In six months, we got a product out, I got interviewed for an hour on an NPR show called *TechNation*, and Apple put us in a software bundle they included with computers sold to middle schools. We had grossed about $3,000 when sales started drying up to about one or two CD-ROMs a week. It was becoming evident that maybe the best we could hope for was to use our CD-ROM to get real jobs, jobs with health insurance, laminated ID badges, and security passes.

Then, in a last-minute effort, I called Kaplan Test Prep in New York. In a series of five phone calls over three days, I convinced them that my 'company' was a viable partner for Kaplan, a Fortune 500 company with millions of satisfied customers around the globe. Together, we could release a line of disposable software (this before the Web could handle graphics, back when it was an unalphabetized encyclopedia of white papers) that helped kids ace their English tests. It was time, Kaplan agreed, to sit down in person. I was in over my head, as usual, but what feedback had I ever been given that I couldn't handle something? I was, according to my dad, ready for a Wheaties box. I was to creativity what Mary Lou Retton was to gymnastics. So I went to New York wearing the one good blazer I had (taupe with a scalloped lapel, strong but feminine) carrying a borrowed laptop and some black and white business cards I made at Kinko's.

I sat in a conference room on the twenty-first floor, chatting over coffee, while we all waited for someone important named Mark, who was running behind. During that short delay, I went from predictably jittery to uneasy and self-conscious. My stomach tightened. I had a sudden chill. My head felt constricted, like I was wearing a hat that was much too small. Then there was another bad feeling, something respiratory.

'Can I get you a coffee?' the guy across from me asked.

'No.' I felt overcaffeinated already, or like I was being electrocuted.

'Maybe a glass of water?'

I was shivering. I could call an ambulance downstairs. Or I could get in a cab and tell them to take me to the nearest hospital.

'We really loved your *Romeo and Juliet* title,' someone said.

'Thanks.' My pulse was galloping. *Was this a heart attack?* My dad's office was only a

178

couple blocks away, maybe I should excuse myself.

'The part where the kids cast the play — that's a great way to get them thinking about what these characters are all about,' someone said.

'Yeah, and teenagers love celebrities, so it's a good lure into the material,' I said, suddenly on autopilot. I'd been having this conversation with resellers, school districts, and software reviewers for six months. 'In the letters we've gotten, students are even more excited about the set design game.' My head was so tight. It was getting worse. Am I sweating? 'Hello, Kelly, I'm so sorry to make you wait,' said Mark.

'Oh, hello, Mark, nice to meet you . . . I understand . . . meetings never end on time.' I focused on Mark but wondered what I looked like. Was I flushed? Was I beading up?

'Mark, we were just telling Kelly how much we liked her *Romeo and Juliet* CD-ROM — ' someone said.

The meeting got going. We talked about a development schedule, a marketing strategy, an estimated budget. I came back from whatever edge I'd been teetering on. After an hour, we stood up, shook hands, smiled. They promised to follow up after discussing it internally. I didn't care. I stood in the elevator and then the lobby and then the fresh air in front of the building wondering what just happened. How long was I like that and when was it going to happen again?

I took the Amtrak home to Wooded Lane and sat at the kitchen table, where I had played quarters with my brothers, where I was grounded for drinking at the sophomore dance, where I read the love letter to my mom. She was at the sink, right where she always stood, wearing her new black work pants, shelling salted peanuts and looking out the window into the backyard. I was afraid to tell her how I had the chills, and then the sweats, how tight my head was and how shallow my breathing got. I was sure I needed testing and an overnight stay and probably some kind of medication.

'Mom, something happened today.' It was a risk, taking this to my mom. She had not soothed me when I was rejected by the admissions director at the University of Virginia or the hiring director at Camp Tockwogh or a popular Washington & Lee lacrosse player named Jeff Mason. In each case, she had said something like, 'That's why you shouldn't get your hopes up.' But this was different. This had physical symptoms. Throughout our childhood, she lived to consult her medical encyclopedia and diagnose our bunions, cysts, scabies, and bronchitis. Illness was her specialty.

'Yeah,' she said, cracking open a peanut.

'Mom, there's something wrong with me and I don't know what it is or how to make it go away, but there's something really wrong, with my head, or my thoughts, or, I don't know, but it is — unbearable.'

She was looking at me with a peanut shell in her palm, seeming almost offended, like 'You stop that talk right now; there is absolutely nothing wrong with *my daughter*. *My daughter*'s head is just fine.'

'I mean, I felt insane today. I felt like I was gonna run into the street screaming. I felt totally out of control, like I was having a total fucking breakdown, and if it happens again, I mean, it just can't happen again, Mom. I can't take it. It was unbearable. I mean, something is wrong, Mom, with my head, and I can't stand it, and if it happens again, you're gonna have to take me to the hospital because they are gonna have to put me under because it's just too much — it's unbearable. I'd rather lock myself upstairs in my bedroom — '

Now she looked scared. She dropped her peanut shells in the sink.

'Well, Kelly, we'll go see someone. We'll call your father's insurance company and get some names of local people to see in the morning. George — ' she called upstairs. 'George, where is your wallet?'

My mom was not generally a believer in doctors, and not just the 'touchy-feely' ones. But she understood that the one thing children need to believe is that their parents know what to do, so she cleared her throat and assumed a tone of total competence. With my dad's insurance card on the table in front of her, she talked to a hotline operator about psychiatrists, a type of medical professional she particularly eschewed. She described my circumstances in generous terms: 'She has been running a small company, by herself, and she has a lot of responsibility. She just flew cross-country to meet with executives in New York.' She was jotting down notes and saying things like, 'And if Dr. Marquis doesn't have any availability tomorrow, whom should we call next? We need an appointment tomorrow morning.' Listening to her talk — her choice of 'we' over 'she' — was hypnotic. I was so relieved I nearly passed out right there at the table.

I spent the next two weeks by my mom's side. She drove me to see two different anxiety specialists. While I sat on sofas describing my symptoms to professionals, my mom waited outside in the car for me, sometimes for an hour. When I said I was afraid to fly, she called the airlines and postponed my trip back to California. When I said I was anxious about my Visa bill, she wrote a check for $3,612.32 without fanfare or discussion of reimbursement. When I said I was ready to go back to San Francisco, she found three panic therapists near my office. At the airport, she bought me a book, two magazines, and a pack of gum. And then, as if she had not already made her devotion manifest, when we hugged good-bye, she bawled.

'If you need me, you call me. I can be in your apartment in six hours. Okay?'

'Yeah.' I hugged her. We smiled and nodded to each other and hugged again. 'Thanks, Ma.' Then, wiping our eyes, we came back to ourselves.

★ ★ ★

I didn't go back east for a while after that. The Kaplan deal never materialized, and although I was out of debt, I had very little coming in. Plus, even though I was making progress in therapy, I was still uneasy about flying and a little superstitious about New York in particular, it being the location of my

183

first panic attack. But my dad was retiring, after almost fifty years of selling ad space, and what had started as a nice office party had grown into a command performance. GT called to tell me that the event had been moved from a large boardroom to the formal dining room they reserved for first ladies and princesses. All the Corrigans were going, and, GT said, if I could get there, we could make it a surprise and wouldn't that be great? I had been to Greenie's New York office many times, I told myself. It was a safe place. I ran through our usual routine in my mind.

I'd sleep over at Wooded Lane. Around quarter to six, the alarm would go off and Greenie would appear in my doorway in his blue pinstriped pajamas.

'Hello, World,' he'd say with a smile.

'Yup, I'm up,' I'd say, lifting myself up on one elbow.

'Don't forget to turn off the electric blanket.'

★ ★ ★

My dad cut things close, no time for breakfast, only coffee. I'd ride to the train station with wet hair, putting on mascara at stoplights.

'Lovey, is that Great Lash?' my dad would

ask, wanting to know if his customers at Maybelline were cutting it with my generation.

'Dad, Great Lash is for eighth graders. This is L'Oreal.'

'The Frenchies, huh? They're good guys, the L'Oreal gang.' As soon as we'd pull into the North Philly Amtrak station, a rundown place where my dad's car had been repeatedly vandalized, he'd say, 'Run over there and tell them to hold the train for the Green Man,' because who wouldn't hold a train for the Green Man?

Once on the train, there'd be at least five people to say hello to.

'Ruth, this is my daughter, Kelly,' my dad would say. Ruth must have been a very serious woman not to have elicited a nickname from my dad, not even Ruthie.

'Good morning, Kelly I've certainly heard a lot about you.'

Then we'd move down the aisle and talk to Ted ('Ted-O'), and Jimmy ('Jimbo'), and a guy my dad just called Elvis, for reasons that were never made clear to me. Each one of them would reinforce Ruth's claim that I was the subject of much conversation.

'Well, you're just as beautiful as your dad said you were.'

'Right. You're the California girl!'

'Ah! Kelly! The world traveler! I know all about your adventures 'Down Under'!'

At the office, it'd be more of the same, starting with Mick ('Irish'), the building security guy, who loved telling me about how my dad once forgot an umbrella, so he borrowed Mick's shabby raincoat for a big sales call. Then we'd go straight to the second floor, to the publisher's office, where my dad would chat up Lorraine, the secretary with the best work space in the building.

'Lorraine! Lorraine, this is my daughter, Kelly Corrigan,' my dad would say 'Lorraine here is basically running the place. Word on the street is that the big guy calls her once a day from the golf course in Bermuda, right, Lorraine?' We all laugh, more at his delivery than his content.

Then Alan Waxenberg would call us in to his stately office. 'George Corrigan, bring that girl in here. I wanna see if she knows where you were last week!'

'Oh come on, Waxie!' Even the kings got nicknames. 'You know I do my best work on the tennis court.'

It'd be like that all day, every time. His favorite person at work was someone he called 'Dr. Wacko,' a skinny guy with a squonky voice whose real name I can never remember. He was fifteen years younger and

Jewish, and all the jokes between them were around those points.

'Your father is like my exchange student. I'm helping him work through his Catholic psychosis,' Dr. Wacko would say.

My dad loved this.

'Lovey, Wacko and I are gonna bring peace to the Middle East,' my dad would say, slightly off on the key participants in the conflict there.

'Well, your father's so old, he probably won't be able to represent his delegation much longer. But you know, when you grow up with John Abbott and Henry Adams — '

'This is his best stuff, Lovey. He just beats it like a drum. It's all he's got on me,' my dad would say.

★　★　★

Clinging to my familiarity with his office and his coworkers, I booked a flight. I knew they'd all be there — Waxie, Dr. Wacko, Lorraine, Irish — and besides, I was sure once I saw my dad, I'd be home free.

I listened to Liz Phair and Ani DiFranco all the way across the country, internalizing their bold, nervy lyrics. About halfway through the flight, I fell asleep. When I came to, I congratulated myself. Drowsiness being the exact opposite of panic, sleeping on a flight to New York was a victory.

I got in early, so I walked around Central Park, practicing my toast until it got too cold and then I sat in someone's dark cubicle, waiting for GT's signal.

Coming down the hall in a silk Banana Republic scarf that I thought made me look professional, I could hear the booming voices of my aunts and uncles and cousins and I was glowing with tribal pride. I was a Corrigan. When I turned the corner, Greenie said my name so loudly that the whole room started laughing and clapping and tearing up while Greenie and I hugged and rocked back and forth and laughed into each other and my dad called out my name again and again:

'Love-E! Love-E!'

Until I became a mother, it was the most irreplaceable I'd ever felt. I had 'made the night.' But then I watched him greet Rocky Shepard and Chris Burch and Betty Moran, and I realized that making people feel irreplaceable was his gift.

After an hour or so, the toasts began. Booker rewrote the words to a poem my dad often recited after a couple beers: 'The Cremation of Sam McGee.' GT talked about what it takes to be a great salesman in America — personal relationships — and how nothing came more naturally to Big George than relationships. I went last and announced that Greenie had been moonlighting all these years at a small organization he started in Villanova, namely our family, and that while we appreciated his fine efforts over the years and had cut back his hours considerably, retirement was not an option. Then Uncle Gene took the floor and brought the room to tears with an old story about Greenie's first job.

'Our mother, Cleta — God rest her soul — was five foot two and fierce, a female Napoleon. Her rule was: if you could walk, you could work. So the first day of summer vacation was no excuse for sitting around on your duff.' Peggy, Mary, Dickie, and Jimmy all nodded in agreement.

'So, one summer, George and I flipped through the help wanted ads and saw something nearby for experienced carpenters.'

As soon as Gene said 'carpenters,' my dad let out a giant 'HA!' Gene pointed at Greenie, like *Yep, I gotcha*, and then went on, expertly holding the room.

'We rounded up some old carpenter's belts and stuck a few tools here and there, and come Monday morning, we were front and center at the job site. The foreman took one look at us and said, 'You guys are carpenters?' Apparently, the tool belts were not convincing.

' 'Yup,' we nodded at each other.

' 'Hmm. Well, you' — the foreman nodded at me — 'go up to the master bedroom at the top of the stairs and get ready to hand out the old boards. And you' — the foreman nodded to George — 'you climb up the scaffolding out front and drop the boards onto the lawn.'

'Easy enough, right?' Uncle Gene said to the crowd, making Greenie double over laughing, thinking ahead to the punch line.

Gene goes on.

'So, I say, 'You got it, boss!' and I hitch up my belt like so and I get up there and pick up a board and walk it toward the window and — no George. So I wait. Still no George. So I put down the board — ' He pantomimes this. 'I look out the window, and as I do, I hear this moan' — Gene moans emphatically for the rapt crowd — 'and there, on the lawn is Brother George, flat out!' Uncle Gene moans some more while the crowd laughs.

'He had fallen off the scaffolding, before a single board had been cleared.'

Everyone howled. The ladies wiped their eyes. People couldn't drink their drinks. My dad held his heart and laughed so hard I thought his fake teeth were gonna fly out. The staff stopped passing trays and just joined the party. GT and I were arm in arm, next to Booker and his wife, Jen, who were the same. My mom was next to Aunt Peggy, who had her hand on my mom's arm, like she couldn't stand it, like she might fall over thinking back to the summer her brothers were carpenters.

Then my Aunt Mary called out, 'Wait, there's more! Tell 'em about the guy who came to the house!' Now my dad had his hand over his crotch like a three-year-old who might just pee right there. My mom kept exhaling and sighing and trying to get a breath.

Gene took over again. 'So the next day, George is at home, a fresh white cast on his leg, keeping it elevated, and this guy comes to the door with a clip board.'

Greenie's laughter had no sound left. He had forgotten this last bit. You could see it coming back to him, like he'd turned to see his childhood dog hurtling toward him across a park. Peggy stomped her foot a few times in early recognition, slapping her thigh and shaking her head.

'He was from worker's comp!'

'Oh, God!' my dad hollered.

And then Gene finished the room off for good:

'So he sits down across from George, with

his pen drawn, and starts filling out the form. 'And what time did you start the job?'

''Eight A.M.'

''Okay, and what time did the accident occur?'

''Eight-oh-six.'

'George,' Gene said, barely able to talk, 'spent the rest of the summer collecting worker's compensation and being tended to by a girl who aspired to nursing or marriage or both. He drove Cleta crazy.'

The night ended with several rousing verses of our family fight song:

C-O-*double* R-I-G-A-N *spells Corrigan,*
Proud of all the Irish blood that's in me,
Never a man to say a word again' me,
C-O-*double* R-I-G-A-N *you'll see!*
It's a name that shame never has been
connected with,
CORRIGAN, that's me!

Greenie capped off the song with his signature move — the leaping leprechaun heel click, which thrilled the crowd even as some of us imagined a broken hip.

The next morning I had to be up and out early. I stopped in to say a quick good-bye to my parents, and there, in Greenie's Merion Cricket Club duffel on the floor of the hotel room closet, were my dad's pants, with a big stain near the zipper, where he'd lost control of his bladder. His boxer shorts were drying out on the doorknob. I don't know when it happened or how he hid it or what it meant, other than he was getting old and things were starting to break down and it wasn't going to be long before his mortality started showing. But rather than play out that line of thinking, I chose instead to relive the end of the night, how the whole room — his sales buddies, Dr. Wacko, Waxie, the ladies at work who saved cookies for Greenie after testing new recipes — sang along with Peggy, Mary, Greenie and his brothers. To me, this was what family was — carousing, demonstrative, and attached at a thousand points.

23

january 2005

Everyone assumes my genes are to blame for my cancer. So Edward and I have an appointment with Gina, UCSF's genetic counselor, to figure it out.

Before we can get out of the house, there's a flurry of calls about my dad. My parents are clinging to a remark a doctor made after he found out my dad was on Coumadin, a blood thinner. The doctor wondered aloud if Coumadin was related to the blood in my dad's urine.

'I think it's that damn blood thinner, Kelly,' my mom says to me, as if tissue had not been scraped off my dad's bladder and biopsied. 'I think he should go off it for a while and see what happens.'

'Mom, he can't just stop taking his Coumadin. What if he starts clotting — in his heart or in his brain? It could kill him.'

'But you know those doctors just love prescribing medication,' she says.

'Whether or not the Coumadin is causing blood in his urine, he's had a biopsy, and the biopsy showed tumors all over his bladder. Going off Coumadin is not going to make those tumors go away. Right? Talk to Schoenberg about it. You're meeting him on Wednesday, right?'

'Yes, Wednesday, finally,' she says, annoyed that it's taken so long to get an appointment at Hopkins.

'Okay, well, he's the boss. Whatever he says, we do. In the meantime, make sure Dad keeps taking the Coumadin.'

'Yes, Kelly,' she says, sounding fed up with my bossiness.

Just as we're getting in the car for UCSF, GT calls my cell.

'You gotta take it easy on Mom. You can't talk to her about blood clots and aneurisms. She's gonna have a nervous breakdown. You gotta tone it down.'

'I hear you, GT, but they can't listen to every doctor they run into. Dad can't just say, 'I've got some stuff going on with my bladder so I'm gonna lay off the Coumadin for a while.' Right?' I plead. 'The thing we're trying to treat is not bloody urine, it's cancer.' GT granted me my logic; the problem was, as ever, my delivery.

'It's too intense; you're too intense.'

Did the situation not warrant intensity? My parents — who were tinkering with prescriptions and making erroneous connections and

195

not taking notes during appointments — were in charge of *my father's* life.

★ ★ ★

'Let's start with your parents,' Gina says. 'Are they living?'

'Yes.'

'Any cancer?'

'Yes. My dad has bladder cancer right now.' Gina's face drops. The pity in her expression makes my throat clog up, so Edward jumps in and asks if there's a link between breast cancer and bladder cancer or for that matter, prostate cancer. Gina launches into a meandering answer that, like much of what we hear from doctors, is just a convoluted way of saying *we don't really know*.

'So, Kelly, what year did your dad have prostate cancer?' Gina asks.

'1992.'

'Okay, and what can you tell me about your aunts and uncles?'

The Corrigan side is massive; the paper isn't big enough to hold all the circles and squares. There's my Aunt Mary and her skin cancer, then my uncles and all their prostate cancer, and then callous, unsentimental Xs over my grandparents. My mom's side is smaller, with only one standout case — her great, unexpressed heartbreak, Tommy.

My mom's brother died slowly and painfully of brain cancer when he was forty-three. After surgery and a chemo regimen that nearly broke him, it was useless. The doctor explained that at this point, it was 'a day for a day,' meaning that a full day of excruciating treatment would only buy him one more day of IV-free living. And so my grandmother Libby buried her only son. My mother worried that Libby, whose best moments were in a church pew, would lose her religion.

'The Catholic church was everything to my mother. I worried that Tommy's death would destroy her. But somehow, her faith survived. It got stronger, even,' my mom said, before pausing and fixing on something out the window. 'Libby couldn't wait to take her last breath. She was absolutely convinced that a choir of angels would carry her up to the kingdom of heaven and take her straight to Tommy.'

When I asked my mom if Tommy's death was hard on her, she said, 'Oh, I don't know,' like she had never been asked that and really, what right did she have to consider herself? 'I guess I figured God had worked things out as best he could.' Then she paused and I almost cut in with another question when she said,

'But later, I'd be playing bridge or tennis and it would feel like something fell out of me, and then I would just think — oh Tommy.' I nodded. I could imagine how something like that could punch you out every so often when you weren't looking. 'Now,' she said, composed again, 'I'm just glad his kids have done so well. I mean look at Little Tommy — ' We all cling to Little Tommy, who is as warm and gifted and unaffected as his father was. Little Tommy lives down the street from my parents and his emotional survival, his palpable happiness, takes the edge off his father's death for all of us.

★　★　★

Gina goes on. 'So, your aunts and uncles, any other cancers or diseases?' Edward looks at me expectantly.

'Um, I'm not a hundred percent sure.' If it were his family, Edward would know. He relishes the little facts; his mind is a file cabinet with a thousand drawers. 'I don't think so,' I add. Edward jots down some questions to ask my mom and dad. Gina nods at Edward, like I'm the spacey waitress at their MENSA luncheon and she's just glad *he's* here.

'We can get answers for you later today,' he says.

'Okay, well, given just what we're seeing here on your dad's side, you're a good candidate for the test,' she proclaims. I notice on her desk a framed five-by-seven of Gina running a marathon. 'The next step is to share my recommendation with the insurance company. The test costs three thousand dollars, so you need special authorization. Of course, you may choose not to do it, since, in some cases, the results lead to depression. But people generally want to know, since the genes indicate a significant risk for recurrence.'

I ask her to quantify 'significant.'

'Well, your oncologist can discuss that with you in detail, but the estimates are between seventy to eighty percent.'

I absorb the hit as Edward follows up. 'Does that mean if Kelly has the gene, she has an eighty percent chance of recurrence?'

Sporty Gina explains that yes, that's what it means, which is why, she adds, maddeningly healthy, 'Many gene carriers choose to remove their ovaries and fallopian tubes, as well as both breasts.'

But I need those things, Gina. Aren't you getting it? I'm a Corrigan, for God's sake. I was born to breed.

We assume I'll get authorization but are willing to pay for it if not, because I'm not coming back here. My blood is drawn, quickly filling three vials. An indifferent technician slaps a patient ID label on each tube and off they go to some company in Salt Lake City that'll tell my fortune in about three weeks.

That night, I have what feels like a long dream about drowning in family-tree symbols, leaving two tiny, blameless, doomed circles rolling around on the beach, oblivious.

'What about the girls?' I say to Edward the next morning before he's even really awake.

'You mean the gene stuff?' he answers, having clearly already been through this in his mind.

'Yeah,' I say, moving closer to him.

'You know, you gotta believe that by the time they have breasts, the medicine will have come so far.'

I imagine Georgia in a college dorm saying to a roomful of girls that her mom had breast cancer in her thirties, and then all the girls nodding solemnly. I think about a grown-up Claire pushing her breast tissue around in the shower, wondering if she feels something new. I think about the forms they will fill out and the boxes they will check. I decide to go check breastcancer.org to see how much I have increased their odds.

'Where are you going?' Edward says.

'I was just gonna check something online.'

'A cancer thing?'

'Yeah, real quick.'

'No, stay here,' he says. 'At least until the girls get up. Lately, it's all cancer, all the time around here.'

He hasn't asked me for something in so long. All he wants is for me to stop. Everyone wishes I would just stop, including me.

'Speaking of which — ' I am unable to suppress it.

'What?'

'Nothing. Greenie's meeting Schoenberg today. They'll find out if it's invasive,' I say, lifting Edward's arm and coming up underneath it. We stay that way for a while, and he thinks his thoughts — my wife is getting better — and I think mine — my dad is probably dying. We are alone, together.

24

On the day I shook Edward Lichty's hand for the first time, we both recall feeling slightly superior to the other. I had a better face, he had a better body. I had a bigger personality, he had a bigger IQ. Nothing much happened that night, save a short mental note about a guy from Oklahoma.

The second time we met, about three months after the first, was in the very same kitchen at another crowded party. I had home court advantage, since the hostess was my friend.

'Hey,' I said, 'I remember you. We met at Meg's last party.'

'Right. How are you? Is it Kelly?' He had an immaculate smile, flawless teeth neatly aligned.

'Yeah, Kelly. Good, I'm good. So that shirt . . . ' I heard myself say, referring to his shiny vintage top. 'That shirt's not you at all. Aren't you from — Oklahoma?' He had really dazzling blue eyes.

'Or Arkansas,' he said with a forgiving smile. 'Same thing really.' He filled my wineglass with just a nod of confirmation from me. 'So this shirt's not me, huh? You don't even know me. I bet you don't even know my name . . . '

'Well, that's true. I don't actually remember your name, but I do know that that shirt's not you. You're more of a J. Crew guy, a business school guy. I'm not buying this retrodisco thing you've got going.' His proportions were excellent — shoulders that made clothes hang right, a smooth front, a nice round tush that sat up athletically.

'Interesting . . . ,' he started as he stepped back from the bar to a small corner where we could talk for a long time. I turned my back to the kitchen full of chattering friends. We were tucked in now, nothing to interrupt us. 'Has anyone ever told you, you look a bit like Monica Lewinsky?'

He had a weak chin and maybe even some acne.

Monica Lewinsky had just made international headlines as the chubby, tacky White House intern who gave the president blow jobs in the Oval Office.

I could have cut him off and moved on to someone else, but it felt like a self-esteem test. Plus he softened it again by saying, 'And before you answer, let me say that you only look like her on her best day, when ten people have been working on her all morning, when she looks great.'

'Uh-huh.' I let him squirm, waiting for more backtracking.

'Seriously. I think she looks gorgeous in those *Vanity Fair* pictures.' He pointed to a copy of the glossy magazine on Meg's coffee table. 'Did you see them?'

It was hard not to smile.

The banter continued — it was clearly working between us — but when the night came to an end, he left without asking for my phone number, and I thought, *Huh? Who does Arkansas Shiny Shirt think he is?*

In the middle of the next week, though, I got a call. He said Meg gave him my number. We went out for a drink, he forgot his wallet, I happened to have a twenty on me, and within a few months, we were, improbably, in love. The sick-to-your-stomach kind, the kind where you smile at the phone after you hang up.

One night, during this brilliant period where I fell in love for the first and only time, we were lying in bed in Edward's crummy little room. In the alley next to his window, a spotlight hung such that his nightstand was lit up all through the night.

'Can you see me?'

'Not really.'

He leaned into the pool of light near his nightstand. 'Now?' he asked.

'Yeah,' I said as his eyes settled on me. Everything was very still.

'I love you, Kelly.' Although we had come so close to saying it so many times, when I actually heard the words, I was speechless. It was here, finally. The rest of my life was finally starting and I was just lying there, staring at it, dumbstruck.

★ ★ ★

That afternoon, my dad was landing at SFO. I think my mom had sent him out to see who this Edward Lichty was. On the way to the airport, I made some final preparatory remarks:

'So, Edward, just remember, when you're talking to my dad, he starts in the middle of things, like he might just lean over to you and say, 'Sometimes, those guys'll try to snow you . . . ' And if he does that, which he definitely will, just hang in there, because he always comes around, he always doubles back and fills in the blanks, so just wait it out.'

'Got it.'

'Oh . . . and remember, he really rolls his jaw around. GT thinks it has to do with his dentures, but whatever it is, he kinda looks like a coke addict. Just ignore it. I'll tell him to watch it.

'And sometimes, he refers to himself in

third person, like 'The Green Man likes his eggs over easy.' And you know, he might burp or maybe even pick his teeth after lunch.' I shook my head in resignation. 'He doesn't even know he's doing it. He's completely outward focused.' What I really want to say is *Love him, Edward, you gotta love him. It'll kill me if you think he's just okay.*

'Kelly. Kelly, stop,' Edward said, smiling broadly and patting my leg. 'It's gonna be great. We're gonna have a great day.'

When we pulled up to SFO, my dad was out front with a tiny suitcase on wheels, wearing his maroon Radnor High School lacrosse warm-ups. But on top of that, since it was a special day, he had added his famous green linen blazer, the blazer I had heard him affectionately address as 'Old Limey' when he hung it up at night. He was grinning and waving and kind of laughing at I don't know what. I shook my head, but a reliable feeling came over me, the one I get when I see him in a crowd, impossibly jolly among the tired, irritated, ungrateful masses. Edward jumped out, arm stretched forward as he closed the gap between them.

'Arkansas Ed! Well, all right!' They patted each other vigorously on the shoulders as they shook hands and then shook hands some more.

'Lovey!' He squeezed his arms around me and we had a long hug. 'How 'bout this timing! I mean, it's like James Bond.' I didn't really know what he meant, but it was funny to all of us, in a vague kind of way, so we all laughed.

Edward drove us downtown to have lunch at Rubicon, a pricey, hip place owned by Robin Williams and Robert De Niro. My dad took the front seat next to Edward while I watched quietly from the back. Their conversation never slowed, my dad occasionally punching him on the shoulder like a favorite cousin or an old teammate. Edward looked back at me every so often with a face of total joy, like he was riding around with Magic Johnson or Bill Murray.

We were seated quickly, and a waiter handed Greenie an extensive wine list while my dad was midstory about a stock tip he once got:

'So, Ark Ed, I'm talking to this guy . . . with ONE EYE.' He closed one eye theatrically, like a pirate. 'THE GUSSER! And The Gusser says to me . . .' He leaned in for effect and grabbed Edward's hand. 'He says . . . Georgie . . . Chicago Rock and Pacific . . . get yourself some, Georgie . . .'

The waiter waited and my dad turned to him.

'Can I get you something from the bar, or perhaps an iced tea?' the waiter asked.

My dad glanced over the list and said, 'You got any of that Kendall Jackson? I just love that Kendall Jackson.'

'No, sir.' The waiter smiled. 'But if you'd like, I could recommend a nice chardonnay.'

'Whatever you say, and can you put some ice cubes in it?' Then my dad turned back to us and shook his thumb over his shoulder at the waiter. 'This guy's gonna take care of business! This guy's got it un-der con-trol!'

Edward, the waiter, and I all shared an amused look, and then Edward said, 'Sounds good to me. Kel?'

'Oh, I'm in.'

And that's how we ended up at a fancy restaurant drinking twelve-dollar glasses of chardonnay over ice.

After lunch, I was finally alone with my dad. 'So, isn't he just the greatest? I mean, is he just so smart, so together, so handsome?'

But my dad seemed to think that his notable résumé and good breeding were relatively inconsequential. He just said, 'Aw, Lovey, the way he looks at you . . . I just love the way he looks at you.'

25

I'm stewing about the ongoing delays in my dad's treatment. It's been six weeks since he was diagnosed.

'SIX WEEKS!' I repeat to GT, who is tiring of my phone calls.

'What's six weeks, Mommy?' Georgia asks, wearing her fleece pajamas with the grippy rubber-bottomed feet.

'Not now, honey. Go finish your Cheerios.'

'But I need — ' She starts again, staring at me with her morning hair and her milky cereal spoon.

'Georgia, go. Cheerios. I'll tell you in a minute.'

'Is that the Peach?' GT asks, trying to derail me.

'Yeah. Look, we've got to get him started on some kind of treatment. God knows what damage has been done since Thanksgiving. My tumor would have doubled in that time.' I find myself doing this a lot — slipping in references to my cancer, to establish seniority.

'Mommy,' says Georgia, who hasn't moved.

209

'Georgia, please!' I snap, turning her expression from curious to tragic. 'Okay, okay. What? Tell me what you need.' I cannot afford a tantrum.

'More bananas.'

'Okay, one second. GT, I gotta go. We'll have to talk about this later.'

This is impossible — me in California slicing bananas for Georgia and Claire, my brothers at work, my parents in Philadelphia tracking down second opinions and insurance authorizations.

'Okay, girls, if you eat a good breakfast and let Mommy make one more important phone call, we can do something special today.'

'What?' Claire asks.

'Chew gum?' Georgia guesses.

'No gum. It's a surprise, and it's way better than chewing gum. It involves paint.'

I owe them this — an hour of my full attention, a yes for all the nos. After all, in addition to being George Corrigan's daughter, I am their mother, and this is their childhood, not mine.

'Okay, Mommy.'

I dial Wooded Lane. 'Hey, Ma.'

'Hi, Kel, how are the girls?' she asks, signaling that she wants to chat about pleasant things we've seen and done, not bladder cancer.

'Good, they're good. So when is Dad gonna start treatment?'

'Well,' she says through a sigh, 'soon, I hope. He's waiting for a form from Schoenberg. And he has to meet the oncologist.'

'So when's that?'

'I don't know, Kelly. This whole thing is just too much. Talk to your father. He's the one who talked to Schoenberg's office.'

'Lovey,' my dad says. 'How are my girls?'

'Good. So what form are you waiting on?'

'Mommy, I finished!' Georgia calls from the kitchen. Then I hear her feet padding across the floor.

'One second, sweetie,' I say, preempting her interruption.

'Go ahead, Lovey. Those girls need you! We'll call you back. I'm on it.'

'So did you take your Coumadin this morning?' I ask, holding my one-more-second finger up to Georgia, and then to Claire, who has climbed up and out of her high chair and followed her sister into my office.

'I will, Lovey. Don't you worry about the Green Man. You just take care of those girls.'

I wish I could. God, what I wouldn't give to stop worrying about my father and just take care of my daughters for one fucking minute.

'Mommy, what's the treat?' Georgia says,

wedging herself between my knees and backing into me.

'One more second, sweetheart,' I say to Georgia. 'Greenie, take your Coumadin. I'll call you later, okay?'

'Can't wait!' he says, like he's on vacation and the entertainment is about to begin. 'Kiss my girls.'

'Okay, ladies,' I say as I stand up. 'Let's go. It's papier-mâché time!'

The girls drag their plastic chairs over to the island. I have a stack of newspapers ready and some boxes from the week's recycling. We're going to make an ocean liner with sails, even though that doesn't make sense. We're using wide blue paint tape to attach two milk cartons back to back for the base when Georgia says:

'When I'm four, can I chew gum?'

'Um, yeah, I guess so. But you're not gonna be four for a long, long time,' I say as I clang around, looking for the shallow Pyrex dish we use for the glue batter.

'I'm gonna be four on my birthday!' she protests, ripping up last Sunday's pristine (untouched) New York Times.

'Right, but your birthday isn't for a long time, like half of a year.'

'I'm two,' Claire claims, tripping the alarm on Georgia that goes off when anyone says anything inaccurate (a turtleneck is not a shirt, a purse is not a bag, and so on).

'You are not, Claire. You are one,' Georgia says while holding one finger up in front of Claire's face. 'One!'

'I'm two!' sings Claire, triggering Georgia's high-alert sirens.

'Mom, tell Claire she is not! She is ONE!'

'Two!' Claire repeats.

'One!' Georgia yells.

Claire answers with a bold, unapologetic swat.

'Claire! Time-out!' I say and point to the hall. Claire frowns as she stomps melo-dramatically out of the kitchen and up the stairs to her room.

'How old do I have to be to have a dog?' Georgia asks, now that she has me all to herself.

I am tempted to tell Georgia that I am allergic to dog hair, a white lie of my mother's that ended the dog lobbying once and for all on Wooded Lane. But I wouldn't mind a dog, someday. After more babies.

'Maybe when you're ten,' I say, hoping she won't hold on to that for the next seven years but suspecting that she might.

After I reach to get the flour and the measuring cup, I call up to Claire.

'Time-out's over! Come down and say

you're sorry to your sister,' I say, starting to wonder if they're going to ruin my papier-mâché treat by bickering.

'Sorry, Georgia,' Claire says on her way back into the kitchen, smiling like a remorseless sociopath. You can almost hear her thinking, *I'll take care of you later.*

We resume our positions — Claire straightening and restraightening a pile of newspaper strips and Georgia cross-examining me.

'When will I be a baby again?' she asks.

I look up and smile. I love these conversations. They remind me of when Booker convinced me that monsters were flipping their long strands of wet, soapy hair all over the hood in the drive-through car wash.

'Well, the thing is, you don't get to be a baby again,' I say, blowing her mind with my omniscience.

'When do I get to be two again?' she says, testing the boundaries of the concept.

'You don't. You don't get younger. You only get older.'

'Oh. Why?' she asks, like it's simple math and not one of the great universal truths, along with the fact that finished basements leak and girls of a certain age are two-faced.

'That's the way it works — for everything. Flowers, dogs, trees, babies. They start out little and they grow. We don't get smaller or younger. We get bigger and older.'

'Then what happens?'

Whoops.

'Well, then, we're all grown up and when we get really, really old — much older than me and Daddy — we die.'

'What's die?' Georgia asks while Claire snips an inch of newspaper into pieces smaller than cut fingernails.

'Die is when you don't get to be here, walking and talking and breathing and eating anymore.'

'If you're not here, then where are you?'

'I don't know. Jammy and Greenie think you go to heaven. But no one really knows. That's the thing. Once you die, you don't ever come back.'

'Oh.'

She has the same look on her face as she did the first time she lost her grip on a helium balloon and watched it get smaller and smaller while Edward tried to explain to her why he couldn't get it back for her no matter how hard she cried or how desperately she thought she needed it.

'But the cool thing about papier-mâché boats is that they last forever. Like in twenty years, this milk carton masterpiece we're making today will still be here. So, who's going to pour the water in the batter?'

'ME!' they say on top of each other.

'Okay, first Georgia, then Claire,' I say, stupidly turning my back to the emerging squabble.

'Mom! Claire hit me!'

'Claire! Did you hit your sister again?' I ask, leaning into her, like she better damn well not have.

'Yes,' Claire cops, because she never lies and she never makes excuses.

'Time-out! Go to your room!' I scream behind her as she trudges back up the stairs. 'And you stay up there!' I bark, probably loud enough for our neighbors — whose house is California-close to ours — to wonder if I eat vodka bars for breakfast. Georgia is crying like she's been whacked with a lead pipe, and Claire is whimpering pathetically like a prisoner in solitary confinement who's finally cracking.

Don't they realize how hard I'm trying? How much I want to be in Philadelphia? How tempted I am to leave them in the kitchen with crayons and Zone bars while I pound out e-mails? I storm up the stairs, grinding my teeth and making my frustration clear with every step.

Claire's on her bed. Her face is wet and blotchy.

'You listen to me, Claire Corrigan Lichty! Hitting is NOT OKAY! Do you hear me? Hitting is NOT OKAY!' NOT OKAY is the expression of choice for mothers of my generation. We use it indiscriminately, for everything from drawing on the table to stuffing the drain full of toilet paper and letting the water run until it covers the floor and heads down the hall.

'If you hit your sister again, I am going to take away bunny!' I am a notch away from Level Ten fury, and it's 10:23 A.M.

'You have a nose,' she says, touching my nose.

'Yes, I do, but are you listening to me? Hitting is NOT OKAY! If you hit your sister one more time — '

'I have a nose,' she says, touching her own nose.

'That's right, you do. But I am telling you right now, Claire, if you hit your sister again, I'm going to take away bunny. Do you hear — '

She reaches up and puts her hands on my cheeks and shakes my face slowly from side to side.

'Fish doesn't have a nose,' she says, sounding truly awed.

'Um, not like ours, not really, no. Fish doesn't have a people nose. Fish has a fish nose. But — '

'Fish nose.' She nods, suddenly seeming divine with her fat, rosy cheeks and gold hair and denim eyes.

'Right, fish nose,' I say, pulling her into me. 'You can't hit people, Claire. I'm sorry I yelled, but you can't hit people. Okay?'

'Okay, Mommy,' she says as she squeezes me solicitously. 'Fish nose.'

'Yeah.' I give up, kissing the spot on her neck under her ear.

I carry Claire down on my hip, hustling to get to the ringing phone. It's Edward, so I put Claire down and tell him the whole 'fish doesn't have a nose' story while Georgia hovers, eager to know what's got me smiling all of a sudden. 'You have a nose, I have a nose,' I repeat. Edward and I are bewitched by our obstinate, nutty kid.

Georgia turns to pour the water into the flour.

'I gotta go, Eddy. The mâching is about to begin,' I say, restored.

I don't think my mom did papier-mâché with me, but I can't say for sure because I don't remember anything before I was five and I saw a green moving van on Wooded Lane, the van that was so big it barely fit on the street. My mom explained to me that a family named the Kellys were moving into Mary-Kay Yancey's old house. I remember being disappointed to learn that Kelly could be used as a last name, and relieved when my mom assured me that I was the only *Kelly Corrigan*. I was just about to turn five. But before the Kellys unpacked, I don't know if my mother yelled like I do, if I ran screaming to her every time a bee bobbed near my head, if I marveled at the masterly way she removed a splinter. I always assume she was a harder kind of mother — intent, staunch — but then, I'll probably seem less snuggly and peppy to my girls when they become eye-rolling teenagers, then condescending college kids.

A couple years ago, my aunt Peggy sent me an old candid of my mom and me on a beach. I look about nine, judging by my supersize teeth. The picture was taken from the side. There's a backgammon set at her feet. My hand is lying on my mom's thigh like it's part of me, and my head is resting against her arm. Evidently, even though we don't touch each other much anymore, we used to. We used to be entwined. I wish I remembered being that way with my mom, being on her and around her and of her like that.

If my mom had died young, like Peggy Taylor in Sydney, I wouldn't have a single memory of her. That's why I take so many pictures and keep old art projects and pull the video camera off the top of the fridge and turn it around on myself to report on the day's events — today we're going back to the park to do the slide again, this is Georgia's favorite book, *The Remarkable Farkle McBride*, these are the sparkly shoes Mommy bought for Claire, who calls them her 'click-clacks.' I was here, girls. Every day. Helping you draw smiley faces in the condensation on the shower door, showing you how to hold scissors and twirl a pipe cleaner and play Keep It Up with a party balloon. This is my graffiti. This is me spray painting on every wall and etching in every headboard: I WAS HERE.

★ ★ ★

The next day, we're getting ready for a playdate.

'You can wear these pants or these pants,' I say to Georgia.

'No.'

'These pants or these pants,' I reiterate definitively.

'I don't wanna wear pants,' she says, staring me down, sniffing for weakness.

'It's too cold to wear a skirt. And I bet it's gonna rain. You *have* to wear pants,' I say, wondering if this is really my life.

'But I don't like those pants. They hurt.'

'I'll cut the tag out. Look, I can just pull it out,' I say, ripping the tag off like Lou Ferrigno.

'NO! Mommy! You ripped my pants!'

'Listen to me, Georgia,' I say getting tighter and more threatening, 'I pulled off the tag so nothing would hurt, so just pick a pair of pants and PUT THEM ON.'

'But — '

'I'm serious, Georgia. Not another word,' I say staring at her.

'But — '

'That's IT!' I shout, throwing her pants on her bed like the irate Russian at the UN summit who has had enough bogus diplomacy for one day. 'You stay in this room until you put on a pair of pants! I am going downstairs and you better get yourself dressed or I'm going to cancel your playdate!'

I pull the door too hard behind me, technically breaking a household rule about slamming.

The irritable, aggressive, demanding shrew that emerged the day my dad was diagnosed is back. She keeps screaming at everyone: THIS IS NOT OKAY! NONE OF THIS IS OKAY!

But then, Georgia comes down wearing a pair of pants. She's smiling tentatively and coming toward me.

'You have a nose?' she asks, betting on her sister's million-dollar line.

'And you have a nose,' I say, with shame and gratitude and wonder.

She finishes it off, 'But fish doesn't have a nose.' I hug her.

'You're the best, Peach. You're a great, great kid and I'm lucky to be your mother.'

And this is why, for at least the next five years, Georgia Lichty will be thinking about fish noses each time she comes face-to-face with her mother's wrath.

26

When I took my first job after college, Big George said, 'Whoa! United Way! My girl — saving the world!' But my mom had misgivings.

'Oh, I don't know about them,' she said. 'Some people think the United Way is like another tax. When I was a teacher in Baltimore, I *had* to give. I didn't have a choice. It came right out of my paycheck.'

'Well, that was your boss's fault. Did you know that United Way gives a lot to Catholic Charities?' I asked her, sure that a link to the Church would eclipse any negative associations.

'Oh, that's something,' she granted.

So ten years later, when a freshly minted graduate from Harvard Business School named Meghan Chen-Williams saw my *Romeo and Juliet* CD-ROM and said she had a start-up that needed someone just like me, I should have known to call my dad.

But I called Edward, my new boyfriend, to make sure he'd be home for dinner. We were celebrating ON ME.

'Eighty-five thousand! Eighty-five thousand

fucking dollars!' I said when he picked up from his desk at a start-up called Teleworld that was paying him seventy-five thousand dollars.

'Wow.' He sounded confused, like I had just told him I had been quoted in *Sports Illustrated*. 'That's incredible,' he said in a literal tone.

'Well, you know, I just threw it out there, and she said that's what she was thinking, and so it's done. I start in a week. So where should we go for dinner?'

'Jeez, I don't know. We'll figure it out when I get home. Right this second, I gotta run to a meeting,' he said.

'Oh. Okay, well, yeah, let's go somewhere great. I'll see you around seven?'

'Yeah, if the traffic's not too bad.'

I shook off his limp response and dialed up Greenie, who immediately gave me what I was looking for.

'Lovey! Fantastic! She's no dummy, is she? Hiring a smart gal like you!'

'You know, I bet I could have gotten even more. I mean, she didn't even hesitate,' I said, having outgrown my fat new salary in less than ten minutes.

★ ★ ★

When Edward got home a couple hours later, I was dressed up and had on red lipstick. I had spent a long time blow-drying my hair, layer by layer, so when Edward got home, it was uncharacteristically smooth and swingy. I had on a little perfume and high heels that made a lot of noise when I walked on our wood floor. I was a girl who wanted to be noticed.

He came in holding the mail. Looking up to kiss me, he said, 'Hey, super hitter.' Then he rolled past me and fell into the sofa and started opening an envelope. I stood in the hallway right where he left me, feeling a little stupid for putting on lipstick and a lot stupid for thinking he might bring home a bottle of champagne.

We had just started living together. A couple of months ago, we were making out for twenty minutes on my doorstep. I had waited for a real boyfriend for a long time, a real boyfriend who would pick me up and swing me around every time I did something new, like in the J. Crew catalogs.

'You got another cell phone bill,' he called out to me. 'We gotta change your calling plan. This should be twenty dollars a month, max.'

A wave of disappointment came sloshing toward me.

'Yup,' I said, 'well, we just doubled our

income, so there's no big rush on that.'

'I guess, but you know,' he said.

I walked into our room and lay down on the bed, partly because I couldn't decide how to handle this and partly because I needed to transmit a stronger signal.

'What are you doing?' he called in. He had missed both the spritz of seven-year-old White Shoulders and the Alanis Morissette hair. Standing in the doorway, he said, 'Kel? Is something wrong?'

'Today was a big day for me,' I started, just to help him understand the general domain of concern. 'I mean, careerwise, it's probably the biggest day I've ever had. You know that, right?' He looked kinda bewildered. 'Okay, let me put it this way: if you got a new job, I'd have made dinner reservations, or gotten you a card, or come home early, or probably all of the above. And you can bet that when I walked through the door, I wouldn't breeze past you and start reading the mail.'

This was our first 'discussion' of this type, the type where I talk a lot and he's blindsided and apologizes an hour later, after the defensiveness fades. I'm never sure if he really gets it or just prefers harmony over retraining a girl who was raised by a man who crowed about her ordinary achievements to strangers on the commuter train as if she had learned

226

to live underwater. Stacked up against such a man, Edward looked positively apathetic.

'I mean, if we're not gonna celebrate this kind of thing, what are we gonna celebrate? Because I'm a fan of celebrations, if you haven't noticed.'

'Well, let's celebrate. I just wanted to open that one bill. Let's go to dinner. Come on. Where should we go? Should we go downtown?'

He tried to nuzzle up to me, but I wasn't ready yet.

'Yeah, downtown is good. But, Edward, is the romance part over? Because I thought it would last longer, you know? I thought I might get more than six months of your full attention before it started to wear off.'

'Oh come on, Kel, I'm sorry. I was distracted. Let's go. Let's go have a great night. You look so nice,' he said, and after a period of ass-kissing and cajoling that I deemed to be sufficient, I let it go.

All in all, by the end of the night, he made the high heels worth it, but knowing what I know now, I should have lowered my expectations right then, since that same spot keeps rubbing.

For years afterward, I'd prompt him: 'So, do you like my new haircut?' or 'Did you see I'm wearing the skirt you like?' Sometimes I

227

even hit him over the head: 'What does it take to get a compliment around here?' A couple years into our marriage, during *Looking for Reaction, Take 17*, Edward finally said it, the thing that lay underneath it all.

'I'm not Greenie, Kelly.' Then he made it worse and better at the same time by adding, unapologetically, 'No one is.'

27

If only I could get to Philadelphia, go to the appointments, see his films. But I have surgery in a week then thirty-three radiation sessions after that. The timing of my own treatment is nonnegotiable. I've asked.

GT gets the e-mail addresses for both of my dad's doctors, Ellis in Bryn Mawr and Schoenberg at Hopkins. I start sending them e-mails every day, asking sophisticated questions that I cut and paste from the Web about tumor penetration and TNM staging, which I don't even understand. I cc Booker, Jen, Edward, and GT, but not my parents, because Greenie doesn't do computers and my mom doesn't want any more information than she already has. Every e-mail ends with verbal tithing.

'I can't thank you enough for your attention and your kindness.' 'My dad is a very special guy.' 'We feel very lucky to have you caring for him.' I want to say, I know you think he's old but he's not old enough, and neither am I.

My dad, although he gave his permission for his doctors to talk to us, thinks I'm hounding Schoenberg. 'Lovey, take it easy on the guy.' My mom thinks I'm insolent. 'I don't know if you should be bothering an MD.' My brothers think I am controlling. 'Shouldn't we talk about it first, before you go e-mailing these guys?' Edward is staying out of it, recognizing a no-win situation when he sees one. But I don't care what any of them think.

My dad's prognosis, which has only been implied in statements like 'This is his *third* cancer' seems to hang on one question: can his bladder be removed? Since the cancer has, as I feared, dug deeper into the layers of fat and muscle around his bladder and crept like mold up into his ureter and down into his pelvic wall, the only chance for a cure is to remove his bladder surgically, after which, he will have to rely on two bags, one for urine, one for the other stuff.

But, Dr. Ellis explains, when my dad's prostate was removed twelve years ago, the resulting scar tissue fused his bladder to the floor of his pelvis, like a grilled cheese stuck to a paper napkin.

'Maybe it can be removed, maybe not. We won't know 'til we open him up,' Dr. Ellis says.

Dr. Schoenberg, at Hopkins, doesn't see it that way. To him, removing Greenie's bladder is akin to 'blowing up a single building in New York City without doing any collateral damage.' It is, in other words, impossible. Not only does he advise against surgery, but he refuses to do it. He urges us to stick to chemo, which has virtually no risk. Other than inefficacy.

But, Dr. Ellis warns us, bladder cancer tends to recur, so we should assume that if chemo works at all, it's probably only a temporary solution. 'I don't know if it'll buy you two years, five years,' he says. Surgery, on the other hand, is what Dr. Ellis calls a 'definitive' treatment. 'No more bladder, no more bladder cancer.'

My brother likens surgery to the sixty-yard Hail Mary pass Doug Flutie threw for Boston College.

'If you connect, you're golden,' Booker says.

I don't really know who Doug Flutie is, but it sounds good. So final. We're all eager to simplify, to break up the shades of gray into particles of black and white so we can organize them into tidy, monochromatic piles and then pick one.

'Chemo, from what it sounds like, is really just putting a finger in the dike. It's just staving off the inevitable,' Edward says, knocking the wind out of me with 'inevitable.'

My dad's chances would be greatly improved if, after all this chemo, he did a few months of daily radiation. But radiation causes scar tissue, which could make surgery more difficult. I e-mail both doctors about the radiation/scar tissue issue. It's true-ish. Radiation will complicate surgery, but will it eliminate it as an option? Maybe, says one doctor. Probably, says the other.

After GT calls Greenie to see where he is on things, GT calls me.

'He doesn't know what to do. He said he was talking to Ricky Graham about it,' GT says, like talking to Ricky Graham, a friend of GT who has no special understanding of bladder cancer, proves that Greenie is as ambivalent as we are. Ricky was probably just at the same lacrosse game as Greenie, and who knows how they got talking or why the conversation shifted from the offense to my dad's bladder. It makes me sad to think about him working through his options with Ricky Graham. I want my dad to use me. But then, I can't help but love it because it's so him — spontaneous and candid and 'hey, why not ask this guy?' (I once watched him ask a Girl Scout for directions to the highway. She got us close enough.) I can just see him leaning over to Ricky Graham and saying, 'So, they tell me surgery's my only chance to beat this thing. Whaddaya think? An old guy like me — bags?'

I try to talk to my mom about it, but I don't like the way she's thinking. I don't even really like it that she has any say in this at all, even though that's absurd and possessive. When I talk about surgery as the only cure, she brings up 'Quality of Life,' which sounds to me like she can't bear to see a tube of shit coming out of her husband's gut.

'GT talked to a guy who had his bladder removed and he plays tennis every week,' I say. 'With the bags.'

'Well, we're certainly not going to discuss *that*. As I've said, it's up to your father.' She always calls him that — 'your father.' Maybe that's why I sometimes forget to think of him as her husband.

★ ★ ★

It's raining again, because that's what happens in the Bay Area. Sometime after Christmas, it starts raining, and it doesn't stop for weeks, sometimes months. It gets to all of us, sooner or later.

'Lovey! More rain out there?' Greenie says when I call him from the car to talk about the radiation/scar tissue connection.

'Yeah, we're into week three now.'

'Boy, I bet those gardens are happy. And those green hills! How are my girls?'

'Great. I'm headed to get them right now.'

'Wish I were there, Lovey. I'd take them over to that place they like — '

'Kindergym, yeah, that'd be good. So, Dad, here's the thing about radiation.' But just then I see an old Asian woman standing out in the rain without an umbrella, waving her arms at me. 'Oh God. Dad, lemme call you back.'

'You got it.'

I toss the cell phone into my tote bag on the floor and pull over toward her. She points to the passenger seat. I let her in, all one hundred pounds of her.

'Souf Baklay Seenya Senta,' she says, pointing and nodding. She repeats 'Souf Baklay Seenya Senta' and assumes I know the way. I drive one block at a time while she points. After a couple of turns, we are lost, going down one-way streets in two-block circles while rain pounds the car. She tells me her daughter 'live in Los Angeles, so fa a-way.' I am at once impressed with her self-reliance and sick with shame that I have left my parents alone in Philadelphia.

How could I still be living in California?

What am I choosing? The food, the collective IQ, the liberals, the weather? That's what I want? More than seeing that doting, giddy side of my mother that, as far as I can tell, only my girls bring out? More than Greenie? What if I've wasted ten years rolling my eyes about social conservatives while blanching organic vegetables and sipping local wines when I could have been confronting the seasons and eating cheesesteaks with a man who voted with the Democrats once and only once, in 1960?

We turn down Ashby Avenue and she points to a big sign that says SOUTH BERKELEY SENIOR CENTER. I pull over to the drop-off point. She pats my hand.

'You good girl,' she says, looking right into me with her milky, gray, old-people eyes. I wonder what she'd think of me if she knew that I only saw my parents three times a year.

I pull away from the center in tears and double back to get the girls, wondering if I should call to say I am late or just focus on getting there. I don't know the number and I can't reach my cell phone so I just drive through the rain, wishing I hadn't been late so many times before. In a few minutes, I pull halfway into the driveway, throw on my flashers, tighten up my raincoat, and walk right through the front door of the wrong

235

house saying 'Sorry but this old lady — '
startling the cleaning woman, who doesn't
speak English. She and I stare at each other
for a minute, me in my raincoat, holding my
keys, her in her Michigan sweatpants, holding
her shower caddy full of Simple Green and
Ajax.

I give up, I say to myself as I fall back into
a fancy wing chair, wishing I could hire
someone less flimsy and pitiful to do my job.

But I can't.

I have to pick up my kids. I have to register
them for school. I have to pack their lunches
and get their Hep B shots and wash their
hands. They must be spotted on the stairs
and potty trained and broken of the binkie.
And if that relentless work runs right
alongside gauging the risks of bladder surgery
on a seventy-four-year-old, well, what did you
think was gonna happen? What did you think
being an adult was?

This is exactly what being an adult is
— leaving a voice mail for the national expert
in urology while scrubbing out the grime that
builds up inside the lid of a sippy cup.
Keeping your toddler from opening the
bathroom door while you inject a thousand
dollars' worth of Neupogen into your thigh so
you can keep up your white blood cell count.
Untangling a pink princess boa while

wondering if you are a month away from losing both breasts, both ovaries, and your father.

My dad calls back as I am driving around the block to the right house. 'All right, Lovey, where are you on this whole thing?'

'Well,' I say, sticking to my original logic, 'all we can do is find the best medical minds and then defer to them. That's why I went to UCSF. If the Hopkins guy says no surgery, then I guess you shouldn't do surgery. I think you gotta go with the best, you know? That's all you can do. Just find the best and then defer. What do we know? We can't decide. We can't overrule the guy who wrote the book. You know?'

'I hear you. I hear you.'

So, that's what we're doing. We're taking the less aggressive route. We're being prudent, which is unfamiliar to all of us, except my mom, who has been lobbying for prudence for decades.

28

The conversation, whether about an upcoming party, a job interview, or a new boyfriend, went more or less like this:

My mom: 'Just remember: if you have no expectations, you can never be disappointed.'

Me: 'What does that mean? That I shouldn't expect my friends to show up? That I shouldn't expect one guy to treat me right? Do you not expect Dad to keep a job and come home for dinner?'

'I'm just saying, you can never be disappointed if you keep your expectations low.'

I considered this a cousin conversation to being 'picky,' something my mom had been fond of saying as my single days dragged on, and something that I interpreted to mean that I better quit overshooting it and take what I could get.

But then there was Edward, seemingly prepared to go the distance with me, and so, having proven my mother wrong on one count, I boldly daydreamed about my engagement. Like, on a hike, I'd pass an opening in the woods and spend the next ten minutes imagining a well-dressed table with lilies and large wineglasses and a violinist filling the air with a sonata and, on my plate, a blue suede box from Tiffany's.

As it happened, in June of 1999, exactly a year after our first kiss, I came home from work to a clean apartment, a man in a suit, and roses. The soundtrack of our romance was playing — Billy Mann, Mike Errico, Richard Thompson. Hmm. Nice start. I got *the feeling*. In fact, had he not proposed, I would've felt embarrassed and even teased. But I was pretty sure where this was headed, so after I kissed him hello, I stepped into the bathroom to look at myself in the mirror and calm down.

I sat next to him on the sofa. We started making out, then, moving from the sofa to the floor, we had sex on a rug my old roommate Ted bought off a chain-link fence for seventy-five dollars. After we had both gotten what we came for, we held on to each other for a long time and I cried, like I do sometimes after a really sensational roll.

Then he said, 'Are you ready?'

While he reached over to pull something out of his jacket pocket, I covered my eyes and kept right on crying. It was a letter, since I am a fan of the love letter, in a white envelope with the little black TiVo man in the corner.

(Shortly after Edward started at Teleworld, a world-class branding team came in and after an expensive brainstorming session, offered up two possible names, Bongo and TiVo. We voted for Bongo.)

I opened the letter. Edward stared at me while I read it. It was typed except the last line, the line that I tried not to rush to, the line that was written in his hand.

'Say it out loud,' I said.

'Kelly, will you marry me?'

'Yes, Edward. Yes, I will. A hundred times.'

After a long hug he said, 'I got you a ring,' and handed me a box.

'Oh my God. Really?' I had repeatedly said I'd rather have a honeymoon than a ring.

'It's not a normal ring. You'll see.'

I opened the box, and there was a square of brushed cotton, bringing me back to a high school Christmas when my mom gave me fake pearl studs, for pierced ears, which signified that, at sixteen, I could finally belly up to the Piercing Pagoda at the mall and get the holes in my ears that God would have put there himself if he had wanted me to have them. Underneath the cotton pad was a giant purple stone, a small boulder really, adhered to a chunky silver band. I thought it was a joke, or maybe candy, until he pointed out the engraved date inside.

'It's the craziest ring I've seen,' I said, laughing and wiping away my tears. 'It's like Kryptonite.'

'You gotta look at the stone. It's called ametrine — amethyst and citrine — which are both pretty soft stones, unless they grow together, which is rare, and then, they are indestructible. At least that's what the guy told me. I had it made.'

I put it on.

'Wow, it's cool, Eddy. I like it. I love it.'

'Clean up. We have reservations. And we're running late. I didn't anticipate the nookie.'

'Where are we going?'

'Put on your black dress.'

As I brushed my teeth and stared more openly at the crag on my finger, I heard Edward whispering on the phone.

'Are you calling Little Rock? Wait for me!' I called out with a mouthful of toothpaste.

'You know what, I think we should call our parents tomorrow,' he said.

'Really? It's not even ten back east,' I said. 'My parents are gonna — '

'Trust me, it'll be more fun to do it tomorrow,' he said, making it clear that this was his show and I should follow his lead.

'So be it.'

As we drove through our neighborhood, I pounded my feet on the space in front of me

241

and screamed out the window, 'I'm marrying Edward Lichty! I'm engaged to Edward Lichty!'

He was laughing while pretending to dial down an imaginary volume knob, his signal for 'too loud.'

'Hey — do Jeff and Michelle know? Did you call them?' I asked, remembering that some of my favorite high school friends were out visiting from Philadelphia and we were supposed to meet up with them tonight. They were staying at Meg's apartment, where Edward and I first met and talked about his flashy shirt and Monica, my doppelganger.

'No, but if you want to stop in and tell them — '

'Can we? Really? Do we have time?'

'Sure. What the hell! It's our night. I can call the restaurant.'

'Oh my God, we gotta run in. It won't take long.' I've always been a broadcaster.

I kissed him a couple times and said, 'This is the best, Edward! THE BEST!' When we pulled up, I jumped out and barreled toward Meg's front door.

I let myself in and ran down the hall, screaming like a *Price Is Right* contestant, 'JEFF! MICHELLE! MEG! I just got engaged to Edward T. — '

Before I could finish my announcement, as

I was nearly falling into her living room, fifty people screamed out 'Surprise!' and in the photograph that was taken at that very moment, my mouth is open so wide a five-year-old could have tossed a softball into it.

I never had another occasion to hug so many people so tight, one right after another, including some of Edward's business school friends, who didn't seem like big huggers. My purple ring quickly became a Rorschach test. Some lifted my hand and saw something hip and original, some saw thousands of dollars saved, some saw a reason to thank their husbands privately for giving them *a real ring*. I came to see it as a symbol of nonconformity, and to this day it makes me proud.

When I got into bed, my body was heavy and tired but my mind was skipping.

'When did you buy the ring? Where should we get married? Did you ask my dad?'

'No, I told him,' he said with authority. 'I just said, 'George, Mary, I am going to ask Kelly to marry me.''

'Oh my God, did you call my brothers?'

'Of course. A month ago.'

'Oh my God, do my college friends know?'

'All will be revealed, Kelly. Patience.'

'Oh my God, there's more?'

'Oh my God, yes.'
'Oh my God.'

★ ★ ★

The next morning, we woke up to an alarm clock I hadn't noticed Edward setting.

He rolled over and said, 'You better get in the shower. You don't want to fly across country smelling like a frat party.'

'REALLY? We're going home? REALLY?' I said.

'Go, cab's coming in forty-five minutes.'

'I need to pack.'

'Done.'

'Oh my God, Edward. You are unbelievable.'

I hustled down the hall naked, singing.

★ ★ ★

We got to New York around four, and by the time we checked into our hotel and changed our clothes, it was time for a drink. We walked across Houston to a place called Madame X, which describes itself as 'a sexy, red velvet lounge.' Way in the back of the front room are warped wooden stairs that curl around to a second floor. A waitress in a Lycra cat suit and pigtails tucked a tray under her arm and stepped aside as I came around the corner. There was a narrow, deep room of people screaming 'Surprise!' Edward put his hands on my waist. I started to make out some of the faces in the barely lit room. Tracy Tuttle, Missy Carr, Ted Logan. Then a voice came shooting clear at me through the noise and the dark and I ran straight into Greenie, and we rocked back and forth just laughing while the people around us held their hearts and wiped their eyes. Even my mom, who was as happy as I had ever seen her, waited patiently while Greenie held me to him and said, 'I knew he was out there, Lovey. A man who loves you as much as I do. I told you we'd find him.'

39

One of the men who didn't love me quite as much as my dad was a guy named John Keady. His mom died when she was twenty-nine, a couple days after he was born, and that made him more grown-up than I am still. Looking back, I don't know how he tolerated my naïveté, my untested, bubbly existence, or maybe that's exactly what he wanted — laughter, inexperience. Apparently, his mother's varicose veins had swelled during pregnancy, and when she mentioned this to her doctor, he said she could have them removed before she went home. Simple enough. But when they put her under, something went wrong — an infection, I think — and she died. John Keady came home from the hospital without a mother because doctors are just people and anything can happen in the OR. That's why you sign all those papers before they put you under. That's what I am thinking about as I pack my overnight bag for surgery.

I've been warned that I won't be able to lift

my girls or maneuver a steering wheel for at least a week, assuming they do a lumpectomy as planned. If they find more than they expect and it turns into a larger surgery, it'll be months. They explain this nonchalantly, like picking up your children is as optional as making béarnaise sauce.

My mom is back in California, having just been here for Christmas, and three times before that. Edward's mom volunteered to come, but my mom won't hear of it. Mary Corrigan knows that doctors are just people, and I am her baby.

She called a week back, on the brink, and I thought, here it comes, the collapse she so deserves, the one she's been repressing for months, the one that should have come back at Thanksgiving, when she had almost gotten used to saying 'My daughter has cancer' and the doctor called to say, 'Your husband has cancer.'

'Kelly,' she says when I answer the phone.

'Hey — '

'Kelly, I am about *this close* to a goddamn nervous breakdown,' she says, sounding every bit *this close*.

Her anger validates me. I am still getting crazy mad almost every day, when my injury is reliably insulted by a small, sharp game piece left on the floor by Georgia, or by Claire, who says she won't wear her brand-new, so cute rain boots that I picked out special for her, since she loves puddles.

Anyway, my mom was finally showing, like an assumed pregnancy that at last manifests.

'These goddamn idiots at the airlines are telling me I have to have twenty-five thousand miles to get a free flight, but online, it says — right here! — that a round-trip ticket costs twenty thousand miles. But of course, when I try to book the flight online, they say they have no miles seats available and — '

'I can fix this. What's your frequent flier number?' I ask, moving toward my computer, disappointed and relieved that she isn't going to tell me how scared and tired she is, how unlucky she feels, how she underestimated how much it would hurt to even think about one single day as George Corrigan's widow, a word whose root, I heard once, means 'empty.'

It doesn't take much to get a flight booked, and I love calling her back to say it's all set, like I'm Glinda the Good Witch. It's the first thing I've done to help her in months, besides not telling her that in one of my early scans two lymph nodes lit up, suggesting that my cancer had legs.

Greenie has had another round of chemo. He says he's feeling 'pretty zonked' and loves teasing us that he is 'all alone, fending for himself.' He jokes that Father Rich'll have to swing by after the ten-fifteen mass to keep him company, making chemo sound about as troubling as a lonely afternoon. I sent him all my leftover drugs — Zofran and Compazine for nausea, Vicodin for bone pain, Ativan to relax, Ambien to sleep. Addressing that envelope was the most useful I've felt in a year.

GT is also in town for my lumpectomy. Booker's back in Baltimore teaching school. He called to tell me he was starting his favorite unit on The 'Stans (Turkmenistan, Uzbekistan, Afghanistan). He chats me up for a while, and it feels good to connect with him.

In the pre-op room, Edward, GT, and I settle in. I get into the bed, and the guys take seats and talk NBA. After an hour or two, Dr. Laura Esserman comes in, her long Stevie Nicks hair tucked into a Betty Boop surgical cap. After I introduce GT and we do a little small talk, I tell her my dad has bladder cancer — a bad case — and that the Hopkins doctor told him to keep doing chemo instead of removing his bladder surgically. I want to know what she thinks. Edward looks at me like *We've been over this a hundred times and the decision has been made so when are you gonna let it go?* Laura promises to get the UCSF expert on the phone, since it'll be a while 'til the OR is cleared for us.

'So do you agree that radiation will

eliminate his surgical options down the road?' I ask, as if she didn't just try to pass me off to her colleague in urology. 'Because if the radiation and chemo don't work, the only option he'll have is surgery.'

GT is silent but Edward can't stand it anymore. 'Kelly, we need to focus on the lumpectomy. That's why we're here.'

Laura nods at Edward and explains to us that her first goal today is to remove and biopsy my lymph nodes, as many as it takes to be sure that there is no cancer there. There are about thirty in all; Laura estimates she'll take five to ten.

'Job number two is to find the last pearl of cancer, that stubborn centimeter that stood up to four months of chemotherapy. Then lastly, we'll follow the lines of what used to be the tumor and remove any tissue along the borders. Everything we take out will be frozen and biopsied on the spot, and we'll keep taking tissue out until we see that the margins around the site are clear.'

'Take as much as you need to. Even if I'm lopsided. My vanity's long gone,' I say. 'And thanks for that phone number — of the urologist.'

Edward shoots me a look, but I don't care. Laura Esserman is famously smart. She could make a pivotal call in Greenie's case. She could be the hero who sails in at the top of

Act V to set things right.

'I just think you need to focus on yourself today,' Edward says, echoing his sister and his mom and some other friends who think I should 'block out everything else' so I can 'go into surgery strong.'

GT nods in agreement.

'Oh come on, you guys. At this point,' I say, looking down at my thin hospital gown, 'I'm just a part in a shop. She'll either get it all or she won't. Do you really believe it matters what's on my mind?' Edward and I continue to talk past each other until a cheery intern comes in to write my initials on my left shoulder.

'Just one last precaution,' she says as she takes the cap off her Sharpie. 'We don't want any confusion about which breast.' I look over at Edward and GT, as if a dentist just leaned into my open mouth with sunglasses and a cigarette.

'All right, that'll do it. We're ready to roll you down to the OR!' she announces, eyeballing us all and capping her pen with a click.

It's time to say good-bye. I try my best to impress upon Edward how much I love him. I kiss him many times and hold his face close to mine and look hard at him and just keep saying those worn-out words over and over — I love you, I love you, I love you — my voice getting higher and higher every time.

He is smiling, like a parent at the pediatrician's office who knows that the shots are gonna hurt.

'I love you too. I'll see you in a little bit,' he says, going to the very heart of my fear.

Somebody rolls me down the hall and I pass a middle-aged patient on a gurney, and she seems totally together, like a real grown-up, which makes me feel stupid and incapable and like *no wonder my family treats me like a baby, I am a baby.*

★ ★ ★

Six hours later, I wake up alone in a curtained space. It's nighttime. 'Hello?' I call out.

A nurse pulls back the curtain and says she'll get a doctor, who appears in short order. Dr. Patel is only twenty-eight. (I know because I asked him.) He reads notes from a chart.

'They took quite a lot of tissue. And it looks like they took seven lymph nodes, all clean on frozen dissection.'

'Okay. That's good,' I manage, awash again in humiliating tears. I can see in his expression that later, he'll refer to me as 'the *emotional* lady in curtain three.'

'Is there someone I can call? Your husband?'

I nod and ask if he can get my bag so I can make the call.

'Eddy?' He's already talked to Laura Esserman. He is elated.

'Clean lymph nodes, Kel! Clean margins! That's huge, Kel. It's all downhill from here, right? I'm on my way!'

Then I call home, to Greenie, who has already talked to GT, who told him everything.

'Lovey! So good to hear your voice. I heard the news. Fantastic!'

I tell him everything he already knows and he just keeps saying 'Fantastic!' like a refrain. I ask about his oncologist.

'That Sandy Schnall — do I have a crush on her! She's a tiny little lady — what a powerhouse mind! Her daughter's in middle school, and apparently, she's a real killer on the tennis court. I'm gonna go watch her play a match tomorrow — you know, just stop by — ' He talks and talks and I smile at the ceiling, crying, thinking about Sandy Schnall's daughter seeing my dad in the stands and wondering what on earth his mother's new patient is doing there. He's so constant, so himself, even as this lethal thing multiplies inside him.

'How about the nurses?' I ask, knowing that they will be his main contact.

'You know, I met a gal yesterday but she's going on vacation. Hawaii, actually. I told her to look for the Green Flash!'

My parents went to Maui years ago, and my dad came back raving about the Green Flash, which he swore you could see if you watched the horizon at the exact moment the sun sets over the ocean. 'It doesn't last forever,' he warned, 'but, Lovey, it's magical.'

Edward breaks through the curtain. He's wearing his Morse College sweatshirt and some old jeans, and all that joy and relief make him look about twenty. The sight of him opens my every emotional pore. All that preop anxiety comes oozing out of me.

'Aw, Kel, don't cry. It's over, baby. It's over,' he says, squeezing my hand.

★ ★ ★

The next afternoon, I'm home again, and everyone's giving me a wide berth, only 'bothering' me to bring in presents and cards. My old college pals Tracy and Missy sent a pot of orange and pink gerbera daisies, because I love them and they remember what people love, and my OB Emily Birenbaum dropped off champagne. Booker and Jen sent a gift certificate for a facial, now that I am 'CANCER FREE!!!!!' My mom's best friend, Betty Moran, sent a flower arrangement fit for a hotel lobby. GT bought Edward a bunch of luxury products from Kiehl's, including this shaving stuff GT swears by. I'm glad Eddy got some treats. For six months, he's been fielding questions about me and guarding my time, like the lead in my entourage.

I am moving gingerly and hiding from the girls, so afraid of their puppyish physicality. Instead, they climb all over my mom, the Marine who lives to serve.

I divide the day between my bed, where I read old *New Yorkers*, and my office, where I read dozens of boosterish e-mails saying 'You did it!' and 'It's over!' And it is over. Everything but removing the bandages and a couple months of radiation. I should be elated, but I can't get there. Not with Greenie in chemo.

Then I see 'Mark Schoenberg, MD' in my in-box. It's mostly a technical e-mail reiterating that surgery is unadvisable and outlining the full chemotherapy schedule, to be followed by radiation, to be followed by a lot of waiting and seeing. At the end he adds, validating my sense of what's ahead and making himself human for the first time in our correspondence:

'I lost my mom to bladder cancer, so I know how hard it is.'

I knew it. I knew this was it.

30

I like to think no one approaches motherhood
gracefully. Personally, I found myself bouncing from self-absorption (Will I be fat
forever? Will I go back to work? Will I ever
see Africa?), to total glee, to heart-stopping
apprehension. My great concern was colic,
which seemed like unequaled hell. I had seen
a perfectly competent friend unhinge completely under the pressures of colic. She
admitted to me during the troubles that
although she was desperate to hear her
husband's car pull into the driveway each
night, she found him grating in every possible
state — smiling or grousing, cooking or
eating, talking or staring, soothing or
ignoring. He even irritated her when he slept.
The sound of his breathing made her want to
snuff him out, like twitchy Othello and
oblivious Desdemona.

By the third trimester of my first
pregnancy, I kept calling Wooded Lane with
new 'What if . . . ' scenarios. What if the baby
won't nurse? What if Edward doesn't bond
with the baby? What if I lose my sense of
humor? At one point, my mother said

something about underwriting a night nurse if it got unbearable, which was my happy-place thought for several days, until I realized that my mom probably thought night nurses cost about fifty bucks a month and, moreover, had always considered my definition of 'unbearable' too loose.

On August 15, seven days after my due date, I stood in the bathroom of our Berkeley rental, staring into the toilet bowl at my passed mucous plug. It was intoxicating. I called Edward and left a message. I called back a few minutes later and left a second message. Ten minutes later, I called the front desk of TiVo and told the receptionist to go find him and then, just to be exhaustive, I sent Edward an e-mail called MUCOUS PLUG, that said: 'This is it, Eddy. Unless you want me to have our baby on the kitchen floor, you better get home PRONTO.'

Within an hour, Edward was home, and twenty-nine hours after that, on my thirty-fourth birthday, I became a mother.

The first week went well. Edward didn't work, but for a phone call here and there while I was sleeping. He prided himself on swaddling the baby like a burrito and exhausted himself trying to trigger a flash of her perfect single dimple. We took a hundred pictures and made daily trips to the photo lab our only outings. We wore boxers and T-shirts around the clock, took phone calls from family, opened present after present and drank a cold Guinness every night with dinner. Afterward, we'd sit in bed, a real live baby between us, and write thank-you notes or stuff envelopes with baby announcements. I produced a massive supply of milk, smug over every ounce. Then Greenie came out to meet his namesake. At my request, my mom was on hold until the following week, for maximum coverage.

'Lovey! Ark! She's a star!' my dad said when he saw her. 'She really is,' Edward said. 'Green Man, wash your hands so you can hold her.'

'You bet,' my dad said. He stood at the sink scrubbing and laughing, I think, because he thought we were being overprotective but maybe just because he was so happy. I remember thinking that if my mother had laughed at our precautionary measures, I would have been livid. That's how it is for mothers.

Edward got Greenie settled into a chair with a Bud Light and the baby. I got the video camera out and turned on Ray Charles. Greenie said he had been telling everyone — Pete Damien at the gas station, Candy at the cleaners, Father Rich at Villanova — that

I named my daughter after him. But, he added, he'd been careful not to brag about the name when Mom was around, because you know, Mary's a nice name too.

On the morning Edward went back to work, I packed three framed photos of Georgia in his briefcase and, waving her little hand, said something like, 'Say Bye Bye Daddy. Bye Bye Daddy.' It all felt so good but also so contrived, like a play we were performing. Even saying the baby's name felt fraudulent. I think all the big moments — good or bad — are like this.

My dad and I fell into a routine within a day. I'd feed the baby while he'd make turkey sandwiches or read to me from the morning paper or bring me a clean burp cloth. Then I'd hand the baby to Greenie, who would hold her against his chest like I showed him and pat her whole back with his open hand and whisper over and over again, 'Heart-to-heart, Peach, heart-to-heart.' We gushed to each other about how well she worked — a burp was like getting a question right on *Jeopardy!*, and every poop was like nailing the daily double.

'Now, Lovey, you gonna change your name?' my dad said one night before Edward got home.

'Never,' I said, leaving no room.

'But what about when Georgia goes to school? I assume her last name is Lichty, right?'

'Yeah. It'll be fine,' I said, feeling unsupported. 'You know why I go by Corrigan, right?'

'It has a nice ring to it, Kelly Corrigan. I'll give you that.'

'No, Dad,' I said, amazed that he didn't seem to know how committed I was to the tribe. 'I go by Corrigan because every so often when I introduce myself, the person says, 'Corrigan? Now are you related to Gene Corrigan from Notre Dame?' or 'You're not George's daughter, are you?' Or 'I played lacrosse against a guy named Booker Corrigan.' That would never happen if I was Kelly Lichty.'

'I hear you. What does Ark say?' my dad asked, frustrating me with his continued interest in the matter and his apparent disapproval.

'He doesn't care.'

'I gotta think he does, Lovey. A man wants a family name,' my dad said knowingly.

Corrigan was my family name, wasn't it? Was he so done with me? I almost felt embarrassed, like I was more attached to him than he was to me.

'Edward is fine with it. You can ask him

yourself,' I said. There was a long pause. 'So how you feeling about your man Bush?' While we were at odds, I figured we might as well cover politics.

'You know, nothing's happened yet. Give him time. He's only been on the job for eight months.'

'He got some tax cuts through, right?' I said, wishing I could be sure it was a trillion dollars' worth and not a billion dollars' worth, wishing Edward were here, since he would know the specifics, like he knows his right from his left. The important thing was that we found our way out of the Kelly Lichty conversation and before long, the baby was awake and Greenie was jotting down what time I started feeding her on the back of a phone bill so I could figure out if she was nursing enough.

A couple days into the week Greenie wanted to 'take a ride over to the new ballpark. It looks fantastic,' he said, holding up a photo of Pac Bell Park in the *Chronicle*. 'Whaddaya say, Lovey? Take the Peach to see Barry Bonds?'

'I guess so, sure. I mean, if it doesn't work, we can just turn around and come home,' I said, thinking this was not a good idea but loving his energy and wanting to be more like him, a real gamer. That's how we ended up in a packed stadium seeing Barry Bonds hit his fifty-eighth home run of the season while my two-week-old sucked on my upside-down pinkie. It went so well we planned more outings — a heist movie with Brando and De Niro, dinner at Garibaldi's on College Avenue, even a trip to Palo Alto to have lunch with Greenie's old friend The Goose, who had been a beach lifeguard with my dad fifty years ago.

★ ★ ★

When my mom came out the next week, the days were much quieter. Her goal was to do everything but breast-feed. When Georgia was not nursing, she wanted me to go get a pedicure or take a walk or read my book. But I was so proud of my baby and all the things I already knew about her — how she always had crud behind her ears, how she liked Desitin in the creases of her thighs, how she could follow my finger with her eyes. I wanted my mom to recognize and applaud my expertise, but my mom wanted to relieve me, so when I'd go on about how to hold her neck or fold her diaper down around her belly button stump, my mom would nod and say, 'Yeah, yeah, we're fine, honey, just go ahead and don't worry about us.' As usual, we were inadvertently offending each other.

I went for a walk every day, leaving my mom alone to tend to her first granddaughter. I listened mostly to a Shawn Colvin album I picked up in New Zealand and have never put down. Where all the lyrics once seemed to be about lovers — holding on, finding communion, suffering long nights of pain — they now made an apt soundtrack for motherhood.

Coming home from a morning walk, I found my mom tucked into a corner of shade on the back porch with the baby on her lap. Georgia was making little noises and my mom was saying, 'Tell me about it. Tell me every little thing. That's it. Go on.' She looked older and younger at the same time. Older, like a grandmother, but younger too, like a girl in an imaginary conversation with her doll. The one image that eluded me was what she must have been like as a new mother.

I knew she was in her twenties and that she lived in an apartment building near Chicago, a twelve-hour car ride from anyone she knew or called family. I knew it was a hot summer because in most of the pictures from that time, she wore flat-front madras shorts that zipped up the side.

Coming up the back stairs, I asked, 'So

does this take you back?'

She didn't take her eyes off the baby. She just shook her head and made a little humming sound, like it was beyond her to describe where holding this baby was taking her.

Later, I was nursing in the living room. The baby was propped up on a pillow, and she had her tiny hands on my breast like it was a bullhorn. Her eyes were closed. She was sucking rhythmically, and I was running my finger along her faint hairline over and over again. I could feel my mom watching us. After a while, I said, 'Did you love me this much?'

She made the humming sound again. 'It's something, isn't it?'

31

(finally) february 2005

I was so surprised I couldn't speak. I just pushed number one on my cell phone and handed it to Suzie Eder, my beloved oncology nurse, and told her to tell Edward, who was in a board meeting but told me to call anyway, no matter what.

'Edward, it's Suzie Eder, at UCSF — yeah, hi. Kelly asked me to call. She's right here. Her genetic test results came back negative. She is not a carrier. No need for double mastectomy, no need to remove her ovaries,' she said, her Brooklyn accent making light of the words. Before I left, clutching the report like a ticket out of Oz, I hugged Suzie, which I had wanted to do since I first met her, probably because she keeps it so professional.

★ ★ ★

'Greenie! Big news!' I say into my cell phone as I merge onto the lower deck of the Bay Bridge.

'Hit me!'

'I don't have the gene!'

'Lovey! Fantastic! Wait 'til I tell Jammy. She's at church right now. I was just running out to meet her. You know, she loves that noon mass at St. Coleman's. Lovey, no gene!'

'Can you believe it? I can keep my ovaries! I can have more kids!'

'Fantastic! Lemme run to mass and we'll call you on the way home.'

'Hey, quickly, when's the next chemo?'

'Wednesday morning, nine A.M. Lemme call you on the way home from God's house, Lovey.'

'Okay, great. Tell God I said hello.'

'And thanks, right?'

'Yeah, and tell him I said thanks.'

'You bet, Lovey.'

★ ★ ★

I envy my dad his faith. I envy all people who have someone to beseech, who know where they're going, who sleep under the fluffy white comforter of belief. I found out recently that Greenie had wanted to be a priest. Well, for like a week he did. He had been going steady with my mom for six months or so when he and his friends Wimpy Lynch and Eddie Wilcox signed up for a three-day retreat with the Jesuits in West Virginia. My dad told

266

me he went for some good healthy intro-
spection and because he needed to cleanse
his soul. When I asked him of what, he said:

'I was a very active young man.'

'Huh?' I said, confused, as usual, by his
choice of words.

'Well, with the ladies,' he says with a note
of contrition.

He told me that the weekend opened with
a fiery brother who impressed him by saying
something like, 'While you boys file in and
settle down, souls are burning in hell.'

The rest of the homilies must've been
equally hardhitting because when he came
back, he galled my mother by suggesting that
he might choose to marry the Church and
not her.

'Oh, I don't know what he was thinking,'
my mom says when I ask her about it now.
'Ask your father. It was craziness,' she says,
shaking off the memory.

But I like this craziness in my dad.

I like it that he's moved by things, that he's
open to unrealistic, even radical, ideas like
abandoning the cushy civilian life to study
with the Jesuits, even though there was no
way they had a lacrosse team, and even if he
could convince them to start one, they'd
probably have to play in their UPS-brown
robes. I like it that he doesn't always dress for

church, because sometimes he pops in spontaneously, like he's pulling off the highway for a cup of coffee. I like how he looks like a boy when he lowers his head to take communion, even now when the priests are thirty years younger than he is. I like how, back when he worked in New York, he'd slip into noon mass at St. Patrick's Cathedral on Fifth Avenue before taking a customer for a seventy-five-dollar lunch at Le Cirque. I like knowing that under his placid surface there is a deep ocean.

A lot of people are praying for me and my dad. I know because the cards we get always say, 'You are in our prayers.'

I remember asking Edward one night early in my treatment, 'Are you praying for us?'

'No.'

'Me, neither. But so many people are,' I said.

'It can't hurt, right?'

Now that my dad was sick, I started to think faith could hurt. Faith seemed okay for everyday, emotional stuff, like being more thoughtful or less irritable, but cancer? You can't pray your way out of cancer. You need scanning technology, and a well-trained oncologist, and a skilled, conscientious surgeon. God's not going to remind your local biopsy technician to check your tissue sample for HER2/neu cells. Your priest can't decide whether you should have your bladder removed surgically or try four months of radiation. Faith doesn't go to the cellular level.

And even if it did, I was pretty sure Greenie wouldn't pray to be cured any more than he would pray for Notre Dame to beat Penn State. He always gave me the sense that the more specific a prayer was, the less chance it had of being answered. So when Greenie talked to God, he probably said things like, 'Hey, pal, thanks for taking such good care of me and my family,' which is basically like giving God a pass.

I asked Greenie the day after my surgery if he ever thought about dying.

'I sure do go to a lot of funerals, Lovey. Lately, about one a week. But that's probably just because I've met so many people over the years. You know, the salesman life. And up at Merion on the tennis courts,' he said, wandering off point.

'So?'

'Well, I'm going to a good place, Lovey. Up there with St. Cleta. What else can I tell you?'

So now that cancer has sprouted inside him for the third time, well, what if the same part of him that actually considered the priest-hood guides him to accept passively what seems to be his fate? I mean, if he really believes in heaven and angels and his mom, what will make him fight to stay here, with me?

This is why I'm crying all the time, even though I don't have the gene, and my hair is growing back, and we're going to Mexico to meet up with friends we don't get to see enough of. Our travel bags get fatter and fatter — filled with stuffed animals and books and rows of diapers, like all we're gonna do when we get there is lie in bed — snuggling, reading, and peeing.

After twelve hours of travel, we arrive and are greeted as heroes. It's so good to see our old friends it almost hurts. We sprawl out on a deck, facing the Pacific. Christy's feet are resting on the side of my chair, and Alec is twirling his daughter's ponytail while he tells us about their flight. Frozen drinks are passed over the heads of six little girls in sundresses and Pull-Ups and in the background, a hip mix plays from Andy and Liz's iPod, because their life in San Diego keeps them in touch with what's young and cool.

Days come and go, and as they do, each person finds a quiet moment to ask me the one thing they really want to know about cancer: what it feels like, or doesn't feel like, what my prognosis is now, who helped me the

270

most, what dumb or painful things people inadvertently said. I love how they listen to me so intently, like I've had tea with the Dalai Lama and he told me everything.

They want to know what I learned and what I think saved me. I tell them I don't feel saved yet. I tell them my oncologist gave me a 30 percent chance for a recurrence in the next five years. I tell them I have no assumptions about seeing Georgia graduate from high school or Claire get married or Edward retire. I say that I'm just trying to get to 2010, the five-year mark, even though the five-year milestone is more myth than fact. In the meantime, I'm trying to do only the things that make me really happy, just in case. I don't want to spend the last couple years of my life dieting or organizing the girls' clothes by season. But I don't mention Greenie's bladder cancer to anyone, and when they ask about him, I look at Edward and say, 'Doing fine.' It feels right to spare them, to keep things light.

On the third or fourth night, a local cook comes in to make us dinner. The long table is set for eight adults. The girls swirl around us like they've lived here for months, eating chips and slices of avocado, sucking on bottles, taking baths together. Joel is playing bartender, tinkering his way toward a masterpiece, which he's calling the 'Brise Caribe.' The cooks put out some snacks, mini fish tacos with some kind of pink sauce that makes the fish gooey and transforms the cabbage.

'So fresh.'

'Put some lime on there.'

'Joel, the Brise Caribe! Divine!'

'Mommy, where's my dolly?'

'Hey, Maggie, here she is,' I say to Maggie, who is threeish.

'Thanks, Kel. Maggie, say 'Thank you' to Kelly.'

'Thank you, Kelly,' Maggie says quietly, to her feet.

'You're welcome, honey.'

'Whose mix is this?'

'Oh my God, is this MC Hammer?'

'Hey, Eddy, where's Claire?' I ask after a quick survey of the room.

'Clairey — ' Edward calls out halfheartedly to mollify me.

'I think that blender makes the lights dim.'

'Try it.'

'Yeah, it does.'

'Claire?'

'Are you looking for Claire?' Andy asks.

'Yeah.'

'Maggie, have you seen Claire?'

'Is Claire in there?' Liz asks the little girls

who are watching Dora and Boots.

'Claire?'

'Did you look in the bedrooms?'

'Claire?'

'CLAIRE?'

'I'll look downstairs.'

'I'll go upstairs to the roof deck.'

How long has it been? When did I see her last?

'Someone go outside.'

'Claire?'

'CLAIRE?'

Jesus Christ. Is the gate locked?

'CLAIRE?'

'She's not in here. She's not in the house.'

Oh God, please.

'CLAIRE?'

'The front gate is locked. There's no way she went out to the street.'

'We'll find her.'

'Georgia, stay here with Sandy and Liz.'

What about the screen door to the pool?

'I'm going to the pool.'

'And the beach! Check the beach!'

'Claire? Clairey?'

Oh God, not the beach. Not the black water.

'Maggie, stay with me, honey,' Sandy says.

'There's nothing to cry about,' I promise Maggie, and myself.

'Claire?'

'CLAIRE?'

'We'll find her. She's probably in a closet somewhere.'

What was I thinking? Coming here?

'Claire? Honey?' Liz calls.

'Georgia, where is your sister?'

'Claire?'

'I don't know, Mommy. Is she in trouble?'

Please. Don't do this. Please. I'm begging.

'CLAIRE?'

'No, honey. We just want to know where she is.'

'I think she's in the bedroom,' Georgia says.

'We checked them all. Which one?'

'CLAIRE! Where's Edward?'

Is this going to happen? Could this be happening?

'Edward is on the beach.'

'Should we call someone?'

'Claire?'

'CLAIRE?'

'She's not in the pool.'

Anything. I'll give You anything. I'll give You Greenie.

'Oh my God, she's here. She's HERE. KELLY, she's right here. She's fine.'

She had crawled into a Pack 'n Play and slid under a white sheet, an hour before her bedtime. With the lights on and the door wide open, she was sound asleep in her white Old Navy sundress, her hair still greasy from sunblock, after a full day playing in the sand and salt water. We had looked right past her three or four times.

I cross my hands over my heart and breathe. No one says much, but everyone looks at one another, trying to shake it off, trying to shake off the fucked-up truth that you might relax for the wrong five minutes and come back to the job to find your baby gone or stone still. The noisy, pudgy, squirming baby that you have loved with a vigilance and wholeness like you've never known, gone. They're thinking, *Shouldn't it take longer? Could it really be that you just stand there in your ridiculous but playful sarong with a frozen rum drink in your hand? Could a child die with MC Hammer playing?*

But I am thinking: *I sold my dad out. Nobody knows, but I traded him for Claire.* Because if it's one or the other, you have to pick your kid.

32

One good visit with your parents can make you want to move home. Add to that a real estate market that makes every would-be buyer reevaluate the staggering price of seeing the sun drop between the two towers of the Golden Gate Bridge and you'll be calling U-Haul.

'The timing feels right,' I said to Edward on the flight back to California. 'I mean, did you see my mother bathing Georgia in the kitchen sink, the two of them blowing bubbles at each other? And how much more can you really get out of TiVo? Aren't you on autopilot a little?'

It was true. After five years, Edward was sleepwalking at TiVo. GT was a partner in the Philadelphia office of Korn Ferry, the largest executive search firm in the world. He had all kinds of ideas about Edward's career, and a hundred people to introduce him to. Although we loved Berkeley, we were tired of paying someone else's mortgage with every rent check we wrote.

With GT's help, Edward zeroed in on a venture capital firm that invested in early-stage companies promising the next 'it' gadget. After a few encouraging phone calls, Edward flew to Philly to interview with six people, one after another. Poking around their Web site that day, I saw something about 'a billion dollars under management.' Mmm, that sounded good. I called GT to find out what kind of compensation Edward could expect.

'Oh, they'll take good care of him,' GT said in a way that made a brand-new Volvo station wagon pop into my head.

Living out west had been fun and it would be neat to hear Georgia say that she was born in California, but it was just too easy to imagine raising my kids in Philly. Greenie and I could go down to the farmers' market, sit at the counter with Georgia in the Björn, and have eggs and bacon. Then we'd run errands together, and sometimes he'd pay for my dry cleaning and sometimes I'd pay for his. Edward could go to Sixers games with GT and Flyers games with Booker. They'd all three golf together on Saturdays and do 5k fun runs on holidays and play guitar for my mother, who loved to hear 'Hey Jude' and 'The Boxer' and all the old Neil Diamond songs. My kids could stay with Jammy on Tuesdays while I went to step class at the health club and again on Thursdays when my pals and I met for Italian hoagies at Joe's Place. Sure, Edward and I might have to teach a few people not to say 'homo,' we'd have to reacquaint ourselves with Off!, calamine lotion, and screened windows. When the first winter came, we'd need to trade in my nearly new VW Beetle for a four-wheel drive. But we could zip up to New York anytime, and our kids could go to Radnor, and we could rake leaves as a family, to say nothing about snowmen, snowballs, and snow angels.

Gary Thomas, a partner at the firm where Edward was interviewing, had played doubles squash with my dad once or twice.

'Ark, you want me to get on the phone with Gary?' my dad asked. 'Go down there and say hello? I don't know him all that well, but it can't hurt, right?'

Edward did not do things this way. He didn't drop in on people, call in favors, or try the back door. It was a matter of pride. He told me once that of all the things he hoped people said about him, he most wanted to be considered fair. Using family connections to get a leg up, while a proven Corrigan tactic, seemed unfair to Edward. Perhaps more important, who knows what Greenie would have said? That Edward was 'a bona fide Silicon Valley whiz kid,' as my dad liked to introduce him?

'No, Greenie. I got it. I appreciate it, but please, I got it.'

'All right, Ark, I'm on standby. Just say the word and I'll ride down there.'

'I got it, Greenie, really.' After he hung up, I promised to reinforce the message with my dad, but only after pleading the case for throwing everything we had at this job search. Edward shut me down.

'If it's the right thing, it'll work out.'

* * *

I guess it wasn't the right thing, because after waiting to hear back from the firm for three weeks, Edward opened a FedEx envelope to find a one-page letter from Gary Thomas saying that after much consideration and internal debate, they had chosen a Boston guy who had ten years of investing experience.

At that point, we weren't surprised, but it still smarted. Edward had talked to so many people in Philly and had come to believe that this job was the only move that made sense. When the letter came, I followed Edward's lead, wanting to get this moment right — to be supportive without denying my disappointment so absolutely that he knew I was faking. When he said he figured this was coming, I said, yeah, me too. When he said he thought the firm wasn't actually that hot, I said, right, if they were, they'd have backed a few companies we've heard of. When he said he thought TiVo was turning a corner, I said definitely, we've always said everyone will have one. When he said we'd better call your parents, I said, sure, but don't worry, they know we'll end up back east someday.

We dialed Wooded Lane and Edward told my dad about the letter.

'THAT DICK!' Greenie said over the speakerphone. 'That's it for him, Ark! He's played his last squash match with the Green Man!'

We laughed, and Edward said something about how being cut off from my dad would probably put Gary Thomas into big-time therapy.

★ ★ ★

Later that night when I tried to brainstorm more job opportunities in Philadelphia, Edward said he had begun to rethink the move, even before the letter came. He said he thought we were Californians now and that we should be careful about changing our life, since we were happy. I sat down on the edge of our bed and looked across at Edward in his boxers.

'Happy is hard to come by,' he said. 'It's

not easy to get all the pieces together. Right now, everything's working.'

'But TiVo isn't working, is it?'

'It's working better than I let on sometimes. And I can always get another job. It'll be much easier for me to get a job in the Valley than it will to find some company in Philly.' He paused. He sounded decided. 'I guess I'm saying that I think the Bay Area is home for us.'

I started crying, which felt manipulative, like I was working him over, but I couldn't help it.

'I'm sorry, Edward. I was just getting so excited to move. I had already packed the boxes in my mind, you know? I didn't know how much having a baby would make me miss my parents. I didn't know my mom would be so into it.'

'I hear you, Kel, but regardless of how much you love your dad and your mom, they're not your future. That's a sobering thing, I know. But that's the truth. This is your future,' he said, nodding to Georgia in her crib. 'This is your life. We're your life.'

33

The way I see it, if you have four kids, you don't really have to do anything else, ever. Three kids is a handful, but one that many people manage to hold. If you're a mother of four, you definitely don't have to have a career or volunteer for the school fund-raiser or even bring an appetizer to the dinner party. In fact, people give you a lot of credit for wearing both earrings and knowing how to spell *chaos* and *antidepressant*. Four kids gives you a pass for every forgotten birthday, overlooked appointment, and missing form. Plus, you can be late for everything the rest of your life and never return phone calls. Who's gonna blame you? It's like having nonthreatening cancer, forever.

It could be that I just want to make it clear that I really love motherhood and I still like having sex with my husband and that I am generally an optimist. You know, the plucky gal who hums along, no matter what, wearing children on her hip in the same casual way other women wear low belts or handbags.

Deliberately having four kids implies that you've got the three-kid-thing sussed out, like there are big check marks next to each name, and so what the hell, let's add another one. It's AP Parenting.

Or maybe it's because I can't believe how much I've learned by watching and knowing Georgia and then how much of what I've just learned is being proven totally wrong by Claire and how much I want to know a few more people that well, *from the very beginning*.

Maybe it's that every kid I've ever met from a big family doesn't take himself too seriously and has learned things you can't teach, like how to transform a pair of hand-me-down jeans into a cool jean skirt with that bandana patch part in the middle or how to make a fort out of plastic bags. Kids from big families make do. They roll with it.

Maybe it's because I want to raise a boy, who will love me all out, like I love my dad, who will love me even when my girls, in pitiless unison, turn their reprobate teenage hearts against me. It could also be that I want to wear those cute maternity overalls a couple more times and eat Oreo cookie ice cream and frozen Tagalong Girl Scout cookies. A pregnant woman eating ice cream in overalls? That's about as buoyant and hopeful as it gets.

Maybe the drama of labor and delivery is calling me back. All that respect and attention. The ever-staggering fact of a real, thriving baby coming from my body, to attend the most ordinary miracle a couple more times.

Probably, though, more than all of that, it's because I am a Corrigan and want to feel like one every day. Corrigans don't stop until they are told to. Corrigans don't sweat details like college tuition. Corrigans don't measure first, they don't read manuals, they don't buy insurance. Corrigans believe.

At every crossroads over the past couple of years, I planned for four. In our crawl space are two giant leaf bags full of maternity clothes that I felt justified spending real money on. I invested in the best breast pump on the market, since the cost would be amortized over a thousand hours of breast-feeding. I picked an environmentally insensitive car that once elicited 'Ever heard of the greenhouse effect?' from an eye-rolling bicycle rider in Berkeley, because it has three rows of seats, for all the kids.

So as my doctor starts talking about hormone therapy, now that chemo and surgery are complete and my periods have begun again, I am missing the disconnect between hormone therapy and 'four by forty.'

It's been twenty years since biology drifted over my head, so it's not obvious to me that estrogen is produced by the ovaries, and never once did I equate the oft-referred-to 'hormone therapy' with induced menopause. When the genetic testing came back and Suzie Eder handed me the report stating NO GENE MUTATION FOUND, I took that to mean that my fertility was not at risk. When Suzie and I were hugging about keeping my ovaries, well, I mean, what's so fucking great about keeping my ovaries if I can't use them?

I interrupt the doctor, making Edward uncomfortable.

'Wait a minute, are you saying I'm not going to have any more kids?'

'Well, we need to eliminate estrogen from your system,' the doctor says, looking at Edward in a way that says, *You know what I'm saying, right?* 'So, yes, no more kids. At least for the next five years, anyway,' he says, still looking to Edward for support.

'But I'll be forty-two in five years,' I say, like he should be ashamed of himself for leading me on.

And then he says the thing that everyone says, the thing that pisses me off every goddamn time, not only because it's Polly-anna bullshit but also because there is no response to it that doesn't make you look like that greedy brat, Veruca Salt, who wasn't satisfied even in Willy Wonka's bountiful factory.

'You do have two beautiful girls,' he said, recalling our first appointment when I showed him the pictures of Georgia and Claire on my key chain.

Would you say 'you do have nine beautiful fingers' to a man who just lost his thumb? Unless you have eight fingers, I'd say you should keep your glass-half-full crap to yourself.

Edward is relieved. To him, 'suppressing ovarian function' is another way to keep me safe, another couple of percentage points in my favor. What does he know? He has one sister and a handful of cousins. He doesn't know how noise becomes music. He doesn't know that five or six people can be moving in and out of the kitchen — doing dishes, wrapping leftovers, picking at the pie pan — and you can feel someone squeeze your shoulders and not even need to see who it is because any one of them is welcome to give you a little encouraging rub and any one of them would. He doesn't know what it feels like to be at a lacrosse game in Baltimore and move from one row to the next, plugging into the family current, cousin after aunt after uncle after cousin, all conduits for the charge, all contributing to the magnetic field until you can practically see it.

For the first time since I was diagnosed, I am seething. I rant all the way over the Bay Bridge.

'Is this what I get? For four months of chemotherapy? Is this my reward? It's unbelievable! I just cannot believe it! It's so incredibly unfair, Edward, so fucking unfair!' I go in circles — this is not fair, why am I being punished, this is such bullshit — while Edward drives and tries to say small things that might help me see it differently without infuriating me even more. 'We knew this was possible,' he slips in. 'They have no choice,' he says about my doctors. 'Fuck them!' I say. 'Fuck them — they don't know. They've never had cancer.' I shake my head. 'They talked about cancer like it was something to get through, to treat, to beat.' They never said it was going to change everything, all my plans, and take things away from me that I have wanted since I was a child. 'They said it was gonna be a *bad year*. So doesn't that mean that when the bad year is over, when you do everything you are told to do — and with a goddamn smile, no less — you get to go back to the life you had?'

Finally, I just stare ahead. I'm so mad and so tired at the same time.

'I thought that was what I was here for — to raise a bunch of kids,' I say as we get closer to home.

The rest of the ride is silent, but as we get out of the car, Edward hugs me and says, 'You're here for all kinds of reasons. I can't imagine all the things you'll do. You're here for me, and Georgia, and Claire.'

'I know,' I say, dissolving into tears.

★ ★ ★

We put the girls to bed and decide to go ahead and call it a night ourselves. As we're putting on our pajamas, Edward makes me laugh so hard by reminding me of this funny, plainspoken guy we once met at a wedding in Georgia. This guy had a chicken named Red who laid five eggs a week, sometimes six, eggs that this guy would cook up and eat. When Red stopped laying eggs, he planned to break Red's neck. Edward said it looked like my days were numbered.

Even though he made me laugh, even though I can hear a joke, I take two Ambien. He watches me swallow them and gives me a sympathetic look that makes me cry again, since the disappointment is right there and has been since I came in the front door and looked at my girls with a mix of gratitude for what is and an aching for what is not. But I've cried so much lately that instead of hugging Edward, I just load up my toothbrush and let the tears run themselves dry.

The next morning, I shower with my girls because they love it and I want to see them smile and hear them squeal. I want to study their shoulder blades and their arched backs and their surprisingly muscular thighs and memorize their bodies because these are the youngest children I will ever have. They squirt baby shampoo on their bellies and soap up my feet and bug each other by barely touching each other's backs. After we get out, I clean a swath of condensation off the mirror and stare at my new chest, noticing the discrepancy between breast A and breast B. A wave of self-pity builds, but then Georgia asks me, in her uncannily perfect diction:

'When I'm four, can I shave?'

I laugh. 'Huh?'

'SHAVE,' she says, louder, like she's a tourist asking directions. Then she starts charading with her hand, shaving her extended jaw with an imaginary razor in careful downward strokes.

'Yeah, I get it. Um, no. You can't shave. You're a girl. Girls don't shave. Only daddies,' I say, feeling the sorrow loosen, feeling like it is possible that what I have will be enough.

'You shave,' she says.
'Yes, but I shave my legs,' I clarify.
'So when can I shave MY legs?' she asks.
'Ask Jammy,' I say, smiling.

★　★　★

Edward is off to Philadelphia again for another work thing. He talked to my parents from the airport and was supposed to have breakfast with them before his meetings started, continuing a tradition that he and my dad have that involves poached eggs, fried scrapple, and the sports page. But when Edward landed, he got a message from Greenie saying he was feeling pretty beat up and that Edward might as well sleep in and go straight to Comcast — it wouldn't be worth the trip out to the suburbs. I had never known my dad to cancel a visit.

34

Once, when I was seven months pregnant, Edward and I were on a street corner in Paris. We had two or three bags each and — choosing to heed the call of my addiction over the sound judgment of my husband, who queried, 'Don't you have enough to carry?' — I had a hot cup of caffeine. Rain came out of nowhere, and every cab shot by, carrying dry and grateful passengers who were tickled not to be us. There wasn't really anywhere to dash into while the rain turned to hail, and well, I just started crying right there on the street corner like a big dumb baby who couldn't possibly cope with the usual travel hassles, much less parenthood.

Maybe twenty dreadful minutes later, after we had thrown our bags willy-nilly into the trunk of a cab and settled into the backseat, my latte nearly finished, Edward said, 'You're not very stoic, are you?' Now, you can only turn down the dials on your lesser qualities for so long. So it was out: I was not 'a tough cookie,' 'a real Girl Scout,' 'a trouper.' I was, in fact, 'not very stoic.'

Regarding my upcoming labor and delivery,

my primary concern was getting to the hospital in time for an epidural. This was my second pregnancy, and since Georgia was born, I had met one woman who had a baby in her bathroom and another who delivered eight minutes after she got to the hospital. This kind of thing seemed to happen with second children, maybe because you get cocky about gauging the pace of labor, maybe because you have to get your oldest kid off to your parents' house. Maybe it's because your innards are still saggy and misshapen from the first time.

★ ★ ★

Stateside again, I was now a week overdue, had gained thirty pounds in the first forty weeks, and three more in the last seven days. I was a classic candidate for inducing. Off I went. An hour into the Pitocin drip, an anesthesiologist swaggered into my room and started to position me for the big needle. In it went, deeper and deeper. The doctor promised total relief in about twenty minutes.

An hour after the injection, both my legs were profoundly numb, but up north, there was a vagina begging for drugs. I was screaming to all of heaven and hell while a roomful of people barked things at me, ridiculous, what-kind-of-fool-do-you-think-I-am things like: 'The only way to end the pain is to push! You have to push! You can get this baby out in fifteen minutes if you just start pushing!'

(As an aside, *just* is defined as 'barely, or only a little' and so has no real place in a delivery room.)

The pain was, forgive me, like being stabbed repeatedly with a long, thick knife.

'I — CAN'T — DO — THIS!' I hollered.

'YES — YOU — CAN!' someone who was not in labor hollered back.

'No! I can't! It's going to kill me!' I cried, sweaty and wild like someone in a bad TV movie. 'I can't do it!'

'You ARE doing it!' Edward said, with a decent amount of conviction and amazement — and awe. 'You ARE doing it! It's coming!'

I dug my now-claws into whatever part of Edward was closest to me and screamed unbridled through an excruciating ten-second push.

'That's it! That's it! Do it again!' ordered a man in sneakers who was staring into a part of me I myself have never seen. 'Again, Kelly! Let's really push this time! Okay, one! Two! Three! Let's go!'

(As a second aside: *let's* implies participation.)

'It hurts too much. I can't do it!' I was blubbering.

'You ARE doing it. You ARE. I can see the head,' Edward said with real hope in his voice.

I made animal sounds and shrieked like a prisoner being quartered, and somehow, this was enough to move a ten-pound baby through my unanaesthetized pelvis and bring the whole bloody mess to a happy ending. It took me twenty good minutes to stop weeping, to stop loathing the medical professionals around me, to stop shaking with shock and bewilderment.

It was then that Edward and I both realized that while I may head straight for the cushions on life's motorboat, when we hit the big waves and the cushions bounce out from beneath me, I can still get through the ride.

35

'Kelly Corrigan!' a voice calls out to me as I cross College Avenue toward Chimes Pharmacy, where I've become a regular.

'Oh my God, Barbara! How are you?' I say, glad that I remembered her name but struggling to bring back her son's name . . . Brian . . . Ben . . .

'We're great! You know, the usual crap! Hosting the inlaws — a total, holy nightmare — up every night with Ryan, who still likes Mommy's boob a little too much. Exhausted, insane, you know. Probably the same at your house.'

'Yeah, I hear you,' I say, starting to remember why Barbara and I lost touch after meeting in a mothers' group a few weeks after Georgia was born.

'Look at your hair! So cute. And so easy. I wish I could do short hair. Brad would kill me; he loves long hair. But it looks so great on you. You have the eyes for it.'

I should explain but she's so chatty and it's such a sunny day. Why go into it?

'You have great hair,' I say.

'Tshh. So, kids good? Still just two, right?'

The 'just' singes.

'Yeah, Georgia and Claire. They're great. Growing like weeds.'

'Good. Good. Edward still at TiVo?'

'Yeah,' I say.

'God, we love our TiVo. We never watch live TV anymore. I don't know how people can live without it. I mean, just last week, Ryan had an ear infection — number seven, thank you very much — and I just stuck him in front of the TiVo and played *Cliffords* back to back.'

'I know. It's the best.'

'Are you walking this way?' she asks.

I was headed in that direction to pick up my prescriptions before going to my daily radiation.

'No, actually, I gotta run to Trader Joe's before I get the girls at their playdate.'

One of these days, she'll hear from someone that I had cancer and she'll put it all together and blanch — her breast-loving son, Brad's insistence on long hair, oh and those seven brutal ear infections. I should have saved her.

'Shoot. Well, we should get the kids together sometime, you know, a little reunion. Is your e-mail still the same?'

'Yeah, it is. That'd be great.'

* * *

Radiation, as one nurse put it, is like 'scorching the earth so nothing new can grow.' I am only a few minutes late, but that's late enough to lose my place in the schedule. It'll probably mean fifteen extra minutes in the waiting room, which is a crowded, chatty place with bad magazines. Pretty Sharon with the salt-and-pepper hair is here. Her twin sister died of breast cancer last year. Julie is here too; she had a recurrence after seven years. When the war stories start, the ones that open with 'I met a woman who had three doctors tell her it wasn't a tumor and then, whaddya know?' I keep my head down. I block out their conversations by flipping through the *People* magazines and evaluating the Angelina/Jen/Brad triangle.

'They said I was only stage one but then there were three tumors.'

Brad Pitt, you dick. How about taking some time off after your divorce?

'Well, at first, it was just calcifications, but a year later, it was a three-centimeter tumor.'

You gotta give it to Angelina. I mean, she is stunning. And she does all the ambassador stuff, which is more than you can say for most of 'em.

'I had breast cancer in my thirties. I'm here

297

now for ovarian cancer.'

Marriage should be illegal in Hollywood.

'Is Kelly here yet? Okay, dear, you're up,' says peppy Carlos, who was probably a male cheerleader at his university.

We talk *American Idol* on the way down the hall — I like Nadia, he likes Bo — and he holds his hand out like a Disney bellhop when we get to the huge white door. It's eight inches thick and four feet wide and the only thing on it is a plastic, yellow and black DANGER sign. I lie on a table, gown wide open, beneath a hulking $2 million machine called a Linear Accelerator. Radiation is a game of millimeters, since right under my breast is my heart. It'd be safer to detach my breast and stick it in a big radioactive dryer for a couple minutes, but bodies don't work like that. Everything is attached, and you have to live with it.

'How are you today?' says the technician, the serious one, while he adjusts my breast.

'*I* am fine. This body of mine is another matter, but *I* am fine.'

'I see you have some burning. Are you using aloe?' he says, pulling the sheet under my back to move me a smidge closer to him.

'Yes, four times a day, but I'm still wearing a bra,' I confess.

'I hope it's not an underwire.' He gently

rotates my arm, which barely changes the position of my breast. 'Just about there — ' he says, referring to my orientation between the lasers. 'An underwire's going to irritate the skin. And it will make the peeling start sooner than it otherwise would,' he lectures, not appreciating that without the support of an underwire, my breasts are two wayward bananas.

He seems satisfied with my position. An assistant taps on a keyboard.

'Okay, we'll be back,' he says as they file out, leaving me there, alone, in a room that brings NASA images to mind. On the ceiling above me, a few of the white tiles have been replaced with transparencies of lush wildflowers.

'Okay, Kelly, don't move,' the voice says through the audio system. I slow my breath. The clacking starts. Sixty seconds later, the arm swings around 180 degrees. I breathe out before the machine's arm settles into the second position. To sneeze or cough or even clear my throat during radiation could put my heart in the path of the laser. Sixty more seconds of clacking. Then the voice says, 'Okay, Kelly. You can bring your arm down.'

Back in the locker room, I pass by a couple of older men in loose hospital pants. They are shoulder to shoulder, paging through *Car and*

Driver and *Newsweek*, waiting to radiate their prostates or colons or bladders. They are Greenie.

I picture him. I imagine the rowdy way he might high-five his technician about the Sixers' win, the expressions he might use ('got the big zapper ready?'), how he might relive the Green Flash with that nurse who went to Hawaii on vacation. I bet it'll be hard to get him to lie still on the table, exposed. Will a technician make tiny adjustments? Will Greenie feel old, weak, close to the grave? Or bulletproof? He told me the doctors warned him that radiation will 'scramble things up down there.' When I asked what he meant he mentioned diapers and needing to stay close to a bathroom. 'Oh, well,' I say. This kind of thing doesn't bother me anymore.

★　★　★

As I walk past the receptionist in the lobby, she calls out, 'Have a great day.' She will not be brought down, and her buoyancy barely escapes being annoying.

'You too,' I say.

The radiation center has valet parking, underwritten by an empathetic patron of the hospital, and every day on my way out, I try to Big George-it with the guys.

'Look at this day, Lou!' I call over.

'Is that a new haircut, Jimmy?' I ask.

Sometimes, when the automatic doors open to the lot's circular driveway and the sun hits me, I even muster up a 'Hello, World!'

* * *

After the second week of radiation, we're on our way to Carmel, for a weekend with some friends.

'We're really getting there, Kel,' Edward says once we get on the highway. 'Three more weeks and you're done.'

'Done what?' Georgia wants to know.

'What?' Claire piles on.

'Done cancer. Can you believe it?' Edward says, mostly to me.

'Yeah, I know. Amazing. I just wish — ' I say, referring to Greenie.

'I know. How much longer until they look in?' Edward asks. Bladder cancer is unusual in that doctors can actually see the cancer and gauge how well the chemo is working. They put the patient under and thread a tiny scope through the urethra, or, as Greenie explains, 'They slip a little camera up your dinger.'

'He goes to Hopkins on April twenty-first.'

301

'He's weathering the chemo pretty well for a guy who's close to seventy-five.'

'I just hope it's working.'

'Well, his spirits are unbelievable. I called him yesterday from work and he answered the phone 'YES, SIR!'' Edward does a good imitation of Greenie's phone voice.

'It's lacrosse, I'm telling you. It keeps him young.' My dad was coaching again at Radnor High, and the season had just begun. 'He told me he had left a message for Sandy Schnall to see if he could do his chemo a day late so he could be at the Lower Merion game. It's insane.'

'Insane or not, he's the happiest person I know.' A fundamental belief of ours — a belief that bonds us together — is that the happiest person wins. 'That means he *wins*.'

'Yeah, he really does,' I said, loving Edward an extra lot right at that minute, on that beautiful drive. It is a moment of transfer — a unit of longing for more Greenie becomes a unit of satisfaction with Edward.

We arrive at Greg and Carrie's just as another couple, Graham and Hilary, are unpacking their SUV. Our girls are asleep in their car seats, like drooling, boneless drunks on park benches.

'Hey, guys! How's it going?' Greg says.

'Great,' I say.

'Hey, we're gonna go for a run after we get the kids settled. Any interest?' Greg asks, disingenuously, since he was probably talking about a fifteen-mile run. He and Graham had recently started doing triathlons.

'Yeah, assuming there's a — what do they call those things — a paddy wagon? Or is it a fatty wagon?' I joke.

Those guys go for their run and Edward swims laps. Inside, Carrie tells us about her flower-arranging class. I take lots of pictures of her four matching kids crawling all over her. Two boys, two girls. I zoom in closer. Their skin is perfect, like suede.

After a couple hours of running, Greg and Graham shower and come out to the deck carrying beers. They have new clothes around their new bodies, tan from hours outdoors, as fit as they had ever been. They have so much to talk about — upcoming races, hamstring stretches, sport socks. They are energized by what they have trained their bodies to do. I am less interested than I should be in their new way of life.

An hour later, two babysitters arrive, and all the women bombard them with vital information about the children. Claire needs her binkie, Rachel sleeps with the light on, make sure Henry goes to the potty before bed. We're off to dinner at a lovely local place.

As the entrées come, Graham reopens the subject of his training. I am quietly drinking my third champagne cocktail when something turns sour inside me. What was disinterest becomes envy, a resentful longing for what they have: confidence. Greg chimes in, saying that last summer he couldn't run more than a mile. 'When was it? August? Yeah, that's right, I was in Tokyo on business the first week in August and I got on the treadmill and I could barely run a mile.' Last August, I was in a waiting room at the Alta Bates Breast Imaging Center, cold with the realization that your body owes you nothing.

'God, I wish I agreed with you. My experiences lately have taught me the exact opposite . . . ,' I say, causing an EF Hutton moment. 'It's just — it's just that I feel such distance from my body — ' My voice is shaky. 'Sorry — but you keep talking about how your body works, and mine, I mean, I have no control over it.' My eyes fill with tears. 'I'm sorry, you guys — but it's just incredible to hear all your optimism, your conviction that you can make your body do all these things. I mean, do you think you can make your body safe? Do you think you can make your body heal?' I can't get myself together. 'I'm sorry, Edward,' I say, looking across at him and hoping I'm not humiliating him with all this sloppy emotion. 'I actually sort of resent my body — oh God, I'm sorry. Talk about a buzz kill.' I don't know if people around us are watching me. I don't know how loud I'm talking or if my tone is ugly or my lips are puffy like Georgia's get when she cries. I need to blow my nose, but the starched linen napkin in my lap is too thick.

I feel different from everyone these days. Words are loaded now — people who were *so sick they want to die*, who ate *so much they wanted to puke*, who hope someone will *take them out back and shoot them* before they get old and infirm.

'Sooo,' I say, blaming it on the champagne, 'maybe it's time to switch to water.'

Everyone laughs, especially Carrie and Hilary, who have tears in their eyes.

'Or tequila,' Edward says.

Everyone laughs again, extra relieved that Edward seems unembarrassed.

'Yeah, then we can start talking about my dad and I'll really lose it,' I blurt out.

Thankfully, no one touches that.

★   ★   ★

Later, when we get in bed and turn out the light, I ask him if my outburst was just awful, if I sounded judgmental or out of control.

305

'Not at all,' he says. Then, surprising and confusing me, he adds, 'I thought it was good.'

'Good?'

'Yeah, it was good. It was real. Those guys could use a little reality.'

I wondered for a minute if this was one of those white lies people tell in irreparable cases, like how all haircuts and babies and new houses are perfect. But then I remembered that Edward can't lie.

'Thanks, Eddy.'

36

About five months after Claire arrived, my body having fully recovered from her searing entrance, Edward and I left the girls at Wooded Lane with my parents and drove to a bed-and-breakfast in New England that I had read about in some magazine. I had stopped breast-feeding, and we were ready to start trying for number three. The Lockmore Inn was populated with pale, wrinkled couples in large sun hats who spoke only in whispers and were there, apparently, to read the *New York Times*, move slowly around the grounds, and then kick back with a Dove Bar in the afternoon. After the second night, when Edward made me guffaw in a hushed dining room by comparing our accommodations to 'The Hotel California,' where people check out but never leave, we called the front desk to say we had to cut our stay short.

'I do hope there hasn't been any sort of emergency,' a man said, sounding just like Lurch would have.

By ten in the morning, we were strapped into the rented Ford sedan, headed south for the last precious night of our vacation.

'New York?' Edward confirmed.

'Yeah, I need a little adventure.'

'Well, if you really want to try somewhere different, we could go to New Haven,' he floated, dying to relive his glory days at Yale.

'I could do that,' I said, essentially volunteering to hear all the anecdotes he could squeeze into twenty-four hours. 'Where should we stay? Should we call ahead?'

Even with all the blue bloods and fancy pants coming through town for reunions and conferences, there are no nice places to stay in New Haven. The Province Inn was the best we could do, well located and cheap. Edward knew it well; his parents had stayed there on many visits to campus.

Before we'd even sat down on our saggy bed, before we'd even adjusted the AC or used the bathroom, Edward was dialing his parents in Little Rock, whom he talks to often, like several-times-a-week often.

'Guess where we are?' he said, smiling into the phone, more boyish than he had been all day, maybe all weekend. While they gabbed like best friends, I unpacked with aggressive efficiency. 'The Province Inn!' He fell back into the pillow, satisfied with their reaction, nodding to me, like *Oh, they're just dying, can't believe it, lovin' the memories of the nights we spent right here in the Province Inn!*

I can't tell you why this bugs me, but God, it does. The way they adore him, the way he blossoms for them, the way he is the most exciting thing that ever happened to them. I know. Ironic, coming from me. I never said I was perfect.

After he finally hung up, I said, 'Okay, well, I've finished unpacking,' as if I was cheesed off because I had to unpack his boxer shorts while he lollygagged on the phone.

'Great. So let's go.'

'Wait a minute. I don't even know where we're going,' I said, as if I was some agenda-happy bitch who wasn't taking one step without a plan.

'Oh, I figured we'd walk around for a while then go eat,' he said.

'Where?'

'Just leave it to me. I got it.'

Talking to his parents had put him in such a good mood, he simply would not be sucked into my bullshit. Other things that made him this upbeat were a good Saturday morning run, tucking the girls in, and learning a new song on the guitar. It was hard, right at that moment, to recall something I did that put such a shine on his fruit.

I stared at him while he folded a wad of bills around his credit card and slipped his phone into his pocket.

'I'm glad you're bringing your cell. If you get bored, you can call your parents again.' Whoops.

'Huh?' he said.

'Do you know that the very first thing you did when you walked through the door was drop your bags and start dialing Little Rock?'

'My parents stayed here like ten times. I thought they'd get a kick out of us staying here, so I called them. It was five minutes,' he said, trimming the number.

'Fifteen,' I shot back, padding.

'There's no way I was on the phone for fifteen minutes. We checked in at — ' He looked down at his watch.

'It's rude, Edward.' I cut him off before he finished his petty calculation. 'How would you feel if I dialed up Tracy Tuttle while you and I were walking around campus? I mean, she and I came up here one time to see her Yalie boyfriend. We could reminisce about that party we went to or how we peed in the bushes behind Marshall Morgan's dorm . . . '

'I wouldn't care.'

'It bugs me that you're always calling your parents,' I blurted out, taking a chance on the truth.

'I know it does.'

'You do?' I didn't realize he'd noticed the way his phone calls home made me pissy.

Edward's parents are on the better end of the in-law spectrum. I had no good reason to begrudge them these calls.

'Yes, I do. And I don't understand why,' he said.

'I don't know either, but when you pick up that phone on a Saturday morning in the middle of breakfast and start talking like you don't have anything better to do, it just infuriates me.' Ahhh, I'd said it.

'Okay, well, most of the time, when I call home,' he said, adopting the measured tone of a seasoned psychiatrist approaching a patient off her meds, 'I have cooked bacon and eggs for everyone and the girls are coloring and there's a natural break in the action.'

I thought it was about neglecting us — and maybe it was partly — but I was starting to see that that wasn't the whole of it.

'I'm just surprised at how closely they track your life. They know who you had lunch with. They know what we're doing on Saturday night,' I said, as if they had been entering the data of our daily life into a spreadsheet for years.

'That's a bad thing? That they care about my life?'

'I don't know. Maybe I'm jealous.'

'Of?'

'I don't know. My parents don't do that. Why do you want to talk to them so much? Why don't you just talk to me?'

'I do talk to you. Believe me, there's nothing I tell them that you haven't already heard. It's not like I'm baring my soul to them and then clamming up on you. You hear our conversations. They're the same every week.'

'So you're sitting there, hanging out with me and the girls, and then all of a sudden, you think, *This is all fine and good but I want to talk to my parents*. I don't get that. It's like getting up and going to read in another room. It's picking them over us.'

I knew I was floundering, but I just couldn't pinpoint why his calls home irked me so.

'No, it's not. It's just habit, tradition. We've always talked on Saturday mornings. Since college,' he said in his I'm-saner-than-you voice.

'Yeah, but admit it, there's something you get from them that you don't get from me. There's a reason that a few minutes after you tell me about your board presentation, you get the urge to call them.' Of course there was something. Of course he still wanted to please them. Of course their reaction was more satisfying than mine. Who was I kidding?

312

'They like to hear about work stuff,' he said, choosing to address only a small part of my observation. 'And yeah, I get something from them that I don't get from you. They're my *parents*,' he said, as if the word alone explained everything.

I shrugged my shoulders and stopped talking. My therapy-loving friend once told me if something really bugs you about someone else, it's probably the very thing you most despise about yourself. I hate the way I still want to make my mom laugh and cry and jump up and down, even though that's not her style. I'm embarrassed that I continue to crave my dad, that his predictable enthusiasm still does so much for me.

'So. Are we good?' Edward asked after a pause. 'How about this: how about from now on, I call my parents from my commute or the office, instead of when we're together?'

'Yeah, good,' I said, wondering why it was all so obvious to Edward.

'Good,' Edward confirmed, moving toward me. 'Let's go. Let's go see where young Edward Lichty got his legs.' We had a conciliatory kiss and headed down the hall toward the stairs because the elevator was out of service. We passed a flyer about the fall semester at Yale, which started in a week or two. 'Welcome to Yale!' it said. It occurred to me that on the master timeline, we were dead center between being the freshman and being the freshman's parents. The idea that we would someday be dropping our girls off at colleges was inconceivable.

★ ★ ★

When we got up the next day, I called home to check on the girls.

'Lovey, she's a star!' my dad said.

'Which one?'

'Both of 'em! Total stars!'

My mom got on the phone.

'Hello?' she said, sounding alarmed, like *why on earth would you call long-distance unless there was some kind of emergency?*

'Hey, I was just getting the update from Dad.'

'Everything's perfect. Don't worry. Go enjoy yourself,' she said, not wanting to contaminate our carefree vacation state of mind.

'I'm not worried,' I assured her, noticing that my mother approached phone calls as procedural requirements, not social opportunities. 'So, have you guys ever been to Yale? It's pretty amazing, I must say.'

'Oh, yeah! It's a great American institution,' my dad said, a street expert in all things great and American. 'Your Uncle Dickie used to coach lacrosse there!'

'I'm going to hang up,' my mom said. 'Enjoy yourself and don't worry one bit about the girls. They are perfect.' Click.

Greenie and I talked a minute but then my mom got downstairs and caught us still going.

'Lovey! I better let you go! You can't spend your vacation on the phone with us!'

On the drive home to Philly, I felt stupid and weird for picking a fight with Edward, like there was something about myself that I didn't understand and that something was now hanging out for my husband to see. Edward didn't bring it up again, probably just glad to have it behind us. But it occurred to me that maybe what was bugging me was that while Edward's parents were holding on and relishing the ride, mine were telling me to change my name and stop calling home so much.

37

april 2005

When you have cancer, or really any big crisis, you find out what people believe in. My mom believes in church and a stiff upper lip and discretion. Greenie says that fresh air, a couple of Advil, and lacrosse can get you pretty far. My Berkeley pals are into yoga, water, and acupuncture. I guess I believe in doctors and research and — after living in California for twelve years — I was starting to wonder about eating right.

Nan Quinlan, the nutritionist I met with before my thirty-third and final radiation session, is an evangelist for anti-inflammatories and antioxidants. Nan Quinlan, you can tell just by looking at her, does not believe in red wine and filet and crème fraîche. Nor does Nan Quinlan believe in produce that comes in cans or freezer bags. 'Flax!' she nearly sings. 'Omega-3s! Legumes!'

'Do you have a notebook?' she asks as she sketches a whole grain on her pad, explaining to me that the outer shell is the bran, the middle is the endo-something, and the inner is the germ.

I don't have a notebook. I don't even have a pen.

'Whole grains are excellent sources of folate, B vitamins, magnesium, iron, copper, zinc, chromium, phosphorus, and vitamin E,' Nan Quinlan reports as she slides a yellow legal pad and a ballpoint in front of me.

Whole grains, I write. Then I add a big check mark, to assure her I got that one.

'Next thing to look for is bioflavonoids,' she says with a smile, savoring each delicious syllable of bio-fla-vo-noid. 'You're gonna love these bioflavonoids,' she actually says. 'Studies show that dark-colored fruits and vegetables have fifty times the antioxidant activity of both vitamin C and vitamin E — so that means lots of blueberries, strawberries, blackberries, eggplant, peppers, broccoli. And they should be organic, of course.'

I write down berries and eggplant and she taps on my paper with her pen and says, 'Broccoli, don't forget broccoli. That's key.'

If any of this were so key, she'd have a handout printed up. If any of this counted, recurrence would be less recurrent.

'Now, let's talk about alcohol. How much alcohol are you drinking?'

317

God, this was a dumb idea, meeting with this tidy, chipper, scrawny, superior — 'Oh, I dunno, maybe a glass of wine a day . . . sometimes two.'

She nods, like a PI.

'Same on the weekends?' she coaxes.

'Yeah, um, more or less . . . '

'Like what would you say . . . for a Saturday night . . . ?' she says, smelling a lie.

Depends who's pouring. Five? Maybe six if we start early and stay late?

'I guess three glasses of wine . . . no more,' I assure her.

'We really recommend no more than one to two alcoholic drinks *a week*.'

Tell that to my parents. My husband. My entire intemperate neighborhood, most of whom are due at my house for unlimited champagne at five tonight, to celebrate the end of my treatment, because in addition to doctors and medicine, I believe parties can be curative.

'Hmm, I didn't know that alcohol played a role in cancer,' I say.

As Nan Quinlan talks about the mice in recent lab studies, my happy thought is that I have to be downstairs for my final radiation in thirteen minutes. How many more edicts can she blow my way in thirteen minutes?

'So, have they seen results in other animals,

other than rodents? Not that that isn't enough for me, I was just curious — ' I say, trying to sound totally open to the teetotaler's life, which I am not.

I am a party girl, a 'one more drink!' girl, a hungover-'til-happy-hour girl. I got this from my people, as sure as I got my brown eyes, my loud voice, and my tendency to touch people I'm talking to.

I am mad, mostly at Nan Quinlan, Messenger, probably because it is so fucking unsatisfying to be mad at abstract ideas like cancer or fate or God. I am mad because this whole discussion suggests that I'm account- able for what happens next, like it could be said someday, 'Well, it's no wonder it came back, did you see the way she ate?' or 'It's her own fault really, she just kept right on drinking.' But I know better. I know Jim Fixx, the guy who wrote the book on running, died of a heart attack while running. I know slovenly, pack-a-day smokers who bury everyone they know and die at eighty-seven, gripping a gin and tonic. But now, somehow, I'm on the hook. I'm liable. And to make matters worse, it's not just me who has to live with my choices — it's Edward, it's my girls.

'The last thing I want you to write down,' I hear her say, 'is organic dairy. This is critical for estrogen-sensitive cancers like yours.'

I write down 'GO ORGANIC!' like I'm on the Pep Squad at Nutrition High.

Nan Quinlan seems satisfied. I am free to take my burnt, peeling breast down to the radiation table one more time. In about five minutes, ten-fifteen is about to be nothing more than ten-fifteen again.

I'm chewing on the idea of responsibility as I lie on the table. I'm remembering how this friend of mine, Kristi, found out at forty weeks that the baby inside her had no heartbeat. At first, it appeared to be a blood clot in the umbilical cord. But the autopsy showed the cord was clear. The doctors had no other explanation; apparently, they often don't. So Kristi blamed herself — missed prenatal vitamins, not enough exercise, too much tuna. She had a rotating list of causes. As long as it was her fault, it was tolerable. Next time, she'd get it right. What made her suicidal was the possibility that it wasn't her fault, that arbitrary danger exists and it can come get any of us anytime it wants for no reason at all.

'Okay, Kelly, come on back here,' says Carlos. He has a diploma for me.

I choke up at graduations, even the ones on the evening news when they compile the best sound bites from graduation speeches around the country, folding in a few zitty, astute kids

320

with the big names like Bill Clinton and Toni Morrison. So of course I cry when Carlos reads my Power-Point diploma: 'Kelly Corrigan, Graduate with Honors!!' I hand him a bag of chocolate chip cookies I made for him and a card that says how his humanity kept me loose and that I'll never watch *American Idol* without thinking of him. We hug good-bye; he calls me 'sweetie.'

I feel like a newly discharged soldier, a kid who was drafted suddenly and shown things she can't forget and then paraded around town on the back of a shiny convertible waving to the crowd of admirers who don't know the half of it. I wear the uniform, I show my scars, I nod through the hero talk. Other vets repel me, and then, just as regularly, they fortify me. Among them I am completely real, not a cancer ambassador, not a patient representative, not 'an inspiration.'

'Lovey!' My dad answers the phone, seeing my name on the caller ID screen.

'That's it, Greenie. Took my last hit ten minutes ago. Over. Done.'

'ALL RIGHT! God, is that great? What a day, Lovey,' he says. 'I'm gonna hang banners down Lancaster Avenue! I'm gonna get a marching band! God, is that great?'

'Let's hold on for the parade until you're done. How're you holding up?'

'I feel good,' he said. He could have been in the ER three times in the past two days, but if he felt okay at the actual moment you asked him, he was 'good.'

'Did you go to practice this week?' I asked, knowing that nothing could stop him from spending the afternoon with his lacrosse guys.

'I tried but I had to turn around. You know what it's like, Lovey, when you're done, you're done. You gotta just get in bed.' He seemed to take a lot of comfort that I knew what he was going through, which of course I didn't. I'm half his age and took different drugs on a different schedule. But I go along with it.

'Yup, just crawl up with a magazine and read 'til it falls out of your hand, right?'

'You got it, Lovey. They think I only need two more rounds of the bad stuff.'

* * *

'You done?' Edward answers the phone.

'Done. Done!' I say. 'It's over!'

'Your last radiation ever!' he says, even though he can't promise that any more than he can change the weather.

When I get home, Georgia is unglued; she can't find the old cell phone Edward gave her.

322

'I have to make a call right now,' she implores. 'I have to call Jammy and tell her that I can chew gum on my four birthday.'

I don't have the energy to search two floors for an item that measures three inches by two inches, so I pick her up and give her a long hug and then I take her shoulders in my hands and find her eyes with mine and say,

'Guess what?'

'You have my cell phone?'

'No, tonight is the party!'

'The last-day-of-cancer party?' she says, looking excited.

'YES.'

'Is there going to be cake?'

'Cookies.'

'Can I have some?'

'Yes.'

'Because cancer is over?'

'Yes. It's over. It's all gone.'

'Can I see?' she says, touching my shirt.

'No, but believe me, it's all gone.'

So goes our first conversation about faith.

38

'I like this house,' Georgia said to our Realtor, Nancy.

'Oh, good,' replied Nancy, who must have been relieved that after months of lockboxes and brokers' tours at least my two-year-old seemed ready to buy.

'I like this house,' Georgia said to me, following me into a bedroom.

'So I hear. How come?'

'It has Elmo, see? And Harold,' she said, pointing up at twin bookcases.

'Well, then we should make an offer,' I said, looking at Nancy like *kids say the darnedest things*.

The wall-to-wall carpet was stained and discolored, like what you see in TV commercials for rug cleaner. Noticing my grimace, Nancy said, 'It's only carpet. If you want Piedmont schools and four bedrooms in your budget, this is what it's gonna look like.'

'I know. I know.'

'And it does have a partial view of the Golden Gate from that one window upstairs.'

'I know, I know.' I wondered how you could spend so much money on a house that has Formica counters and linoleum floors in the kitchen, a buckling deck that you'd be afraid to jump rope on, and plastic shower stalls. 'Maybe we won't have four kids. Maybe we'll stop trying for number three and take that remodeled two-bedroom on Palm.'

Nancy looked at me with raised eyebrows, like maybe that wasn't such a bad idea.

'I'm kidding. I gotta have four. It's in my DNA,' I said.

'Bids are due by eight tomorrow night.' Nancy's phone rang and she stepped away.

Georgia pointed to *Harold and the Purple Crayon*.

'Read.'

'Read what?'

'Read, please.'

So I pulled it off the shelf and sat down next to Claire in her bucket car seat.

There was little, overconfident Harold in his Union Suit wandering around with nothing but a crayon. First he's high on adventure, then he's scratching his head and trying to figure out how he got so far from home, and then he's imagining a picnic blanket covered with pies.

Piedmont had famously good schools, movies outside in the park during the summer, and a rec department where the girls could take carpentry, Japanese, and fencing, not to mention pedestrian pursuits like soccer and gymnastics.

'He's lost, Mommy,' Georgia said, smiling, knowing he would figure it out.

The house needed a new kitchen. The bathrooms were grim. But Nancy kept saying, 'You always have to give up something.' Just getting new appliances — maybe I could talk my mom into a loan — am I too old to take money from my mother?

There goes Harold, starting to crack, retracing his steps, free-falling.

If we bought this house, we'd be giving up Wooded Lane.

'Where is his window?' Georgia asked.

We'd be twenty minutes from the Oakland airport, which had recently announced direct flights to Philadelphia on Southwest. The bedroom in the basement would be perfect for my parents.

'Right there,' I pointed. 'Right where he drew it.' I snapped the book closed.

'Again,' Georgia said automatically.

'No,' I said automatically.

'Please!'

Nancy leaned in and gave me the one-more-second finger, so I gave in.

'Okay, one more time.'

★ ★ ★

326

I e-mailed my mom the link to the listing in the morning. In the online 'Photo Tour,' the house looked magnificent, when really it was more 'cute.' My mom liked how bright it was and kept saying how nice it would be for Edward to ride the train; she worried about all that driving he did. Greenie gave the house a hearty endorsement. But neither of them made a single remark about how far it was from Wooded Lane, even when I talked about the guest room.

'It's in the basement and it has its own bathroom, so you can just unpack all your stuff and leave your razor in the shower and the girls won't touch any of it,' I promised. 'And the best thing is you can't hear the baby crying from down there.'

'Sure, Lovey! Sounds great!' my dad said. 'Or we can stay at that place down the hill with the tennis courts. What's it called? The Claremont?'

'Yeah, The Claremont, but you won't have to. That's what I'm saying. If we buy this house, you'll have your own space. Tell Mom I'll even get her a pillow for her hair.' My mom usually packed her pillow on her trips to California; she swore her special silk pillowcase extended the life of her hairdo.

'Sure! Whatever you say, Lovey!' he said, like it was all the same to him — The

Claremont, the guest room, whatever.

'Kel?' My mom had picked up. 'It looks terrific.'

'I was just telling Dad about the guest room. You can have your own floor to yourself.' My mother often wondered aloud if Edward really wanted to see his mother-in-law walking around in her bathrobe.

But she redirected me: 'It has good schools, that's the important thing.'

Yeah, that was what was important. That's what we were doing — buying a house for our kids, a house where my parents, who were once the central force of my life, would come stay in the basement, as guests.

39

I had imagined bringing flowers or cookies, but when the day comes to meet Greenie's doctors, I feel corny about it, so I show up at his Infusion Center empty-handed. Sandy Schnall, who's just as tiny as my dad said she was, hugs me, and I squeeze her back.

'I just can't thank you — '

'Your dad's a special guy,' she says in her unassuming Philly accent. She reminds me of Claudia, one of Georgia's preschool teachers, whom I also had a hard time thanking enough.

'Yup,' I nod as we smile at each other. 'So, do you think it's working?' I ask, even though I know she has no way of knowing.

'Hopefully.'

'Lovey! Come on back here and meet my gang!' Greenie calls out from his seat, tethered by his IV.

Just like every other place he has ever paraded me around — his office, a lacrosse field, the farmers' market — everyone already knows a lot about me.

'All finished with your treatment?' says a lady in a blondish wig that's too bouncy for her tired face.

'Now, how are those adorable girls of yours? Your dad just raves about them!' says an older woman in a lavender and white houndstooth turban that I think must be available only on the Main Line.

'Why, you're just as pretty as he said you were!' says a bald guy, lowering his book of a thousand crossword puzzles.

It's just like UCSF — the oversize reclining chairs, the staff moving efficiently among the patients, the sense of order and purpose and camaraderie.

After some chatting about the NBA playoffs, Greenie says he's just gonna 'slide back for a few minutes of shut-eye,' which translates to 'I'm gonna take a two-hour nap.' So, after I arrange a blanket around his feet and put his beat-up Docksiders neatly beside his bag, and stare at him a little, I decide to go check on the girls.

When I get back to Wooded Lane, there's a note from Edward on the kitchen table.

'At park. Call if you need me. E'

I turn to the morning dishes. Most of the bowls have been chipped, and every spoon has been bounced around in the disposal. I put away a frying pan and notice some rust in the joint near the handle. The pot holders are stained and thin and look about ten years old, which is not quite as old as the dish towels look. Over the sink, a couple photos are displayed across the windowsill, which is sweet, but the photos have been cut such that they don't entirely fill the opening and the 'brass' drugstore frames are chipping.

In the bathroom, there are more signs of age. Random towels fight for space on the rack — a couple are linen, one's mono-grammed, another is thick enough to dry an entire body. The toilet seat slides to the left. The snapshot on the homemade shelf in front of me is dark and fuzzy and stamped with the date in those futuristic digital numbers that you see on alarm clocks.

Ten minutes later, I am wheeling through Bed, Bath & Beyond with a cart full of new silverware, dishes, dish towels, and pots. When I get to the section where they sell sponges, scrub brushes, and soap dispensers, I toss in some of those. I wander around, looking for whatever else might revive Wooded Lane. Sixty minutes later, I leave with new bath mats, a linen shower curtain and liner, a set of blue bath towels and twelve white wooden frames of various sizes. I am buzzing with do-gooder-ness as I fill the trunk of Greenie's car with $412 of untainted newness and head back to pick him up at chemo.

'That was great, Lovey' — he settles into the passenger seat like a lounge chair, not touching the seat belt — 'having you there, seeing my ladies in the back, meeting my girlfriend, Sandy Schnall. I mean, is she a doll? She's a doll,' he answers his own question.

'She's great. I always wanted you to meet my UCSF people.'

'Sure!' he says, like he can't believe he didn't think of it himself. 'We'll do it the next time I come out! Terrific!'

'Yeah. My gal, Catherine, and Suzie. Oh and Irish Pauline . . . you'll love 'em.'

'Irish Pauline! We'll have to tell her about our trip to the Old Country! Where's she from?'

'I think County Clare.'

'Those ladies are angels, Lovey.'

'The chemo nurses?' I ask, to confirm that we're still talking about nurses, because we may be talking about barmaids in County Clare or the women at the airlines who found his luggage in Dublin or really any group of women that has anything to do with travel, Ireland, or cancer.

'Yeah,' he says. 'Unbelievable. So, Lovey,' he says as we drive past the Kellys' house and

332

close in on the cul-de-sac. 'Here's what I'm gonna do: I'm gonna hit the fart sack for a few minutes and then bang-o! I'll be ready for my girls!'

'Okay,' I say, laughing. *Who calls a bed a 'fart sack'?*

The house is still empty. Edward's probably making work calls from the bench by the play structure, holding out the occasional thumbs-up when Claire crawls through the tunnel or Georgia comes down the slide. My mom won't be back until five, since today is her big bridge match.

I watch Greenie on the stairs, pulling on the railing, with a *Sports Illustrated* folded longways in his back pocket. I see lots of pink skin between the thinning white strands of his hair. It looks brittle, like a dried-up house plant. After following him with a big glass of water for his nightstand, I watch him sink into an old mattress with a sigh.

'All right, Lovey,' he says, 'I'll see you on the other side.'

I watch him tuck himself in, under a polyester bedspread that doesn't seem up to the job. Near the top of the sheets, where my dad's head is, my mom has written MASTER DOUBLE, right on the fabric, with a Sharpie, I suppose so she can tell which sheets are which when they're stacked in the linen closet. The elastic on the fitted bottom sheet is hanging off the corner.

While Greenie rests, I unpack my purchases and manically peel off stickers and cut off price tags and switch things out like I am on a TV makeover show where the goal is to make as many enhancements as you can in twenty minutes. In a growing row of brown grocery bags are eleven scuffed Lucite frames, four ratty snapshots, six spoons, seven forks, five knives, a dusty arrangement of silk flowers, a mounted poster of an owl, a white eyelet shower curtain with a water stain across the bottom, two bath mats, a mismatched set of dishes, five pot holders of various colors and types, a poster of dogs playing bridge (or poker), and three hand towels.

I am high on productivity when I hear Edward saying, 'I bet she is. I bet when you open that door — Clairey, keep moving — I bet when you open that door, Mommy is going to be inside.'

'MOMMY!'

'What are you doing?' Edward asks, in the dubious tone that he always denies and I always hate.

'Just blowing a little life into things. Look at these frames — they all match, *and* all the pictures fit right. *And regardez!*' I say, waving my hand over the utensil drawer like a French *The Price Is Right* babe. 'Wait 'til you see the bathroom upstairs! Hi, Clairey. Hi, Peach,' I say, looking down at the girls standing on top of my feet like they've started to do lately.

'What's in the bathroom?' Georgia asks, probably imagining presents or helium balloons or something better than a new khaki bath mat by Ralph Lauren Home.

'Hey girls, I think I just heard Jammy's car!'

'JAMMY!'

'Keep her in the laundry room for a second. Lemme get these bags out of here. I want to give the grand tour!' I say to the girls.

'Jammy! Mommy got you pictures!' Georgia says, before my mom even steps into the laundry room.

'She did?'

'You can't go in there yet!' Georgia is thrilled to be in the know.

'Okay!' I call out. 'Enter!'

'What's going on?' she says, smiling. 'Where's your father?'

'He's napping. Okay. So. I did a little spring cleaning. Look around. See if you notice any changes,' I say, simpering.

'Well, I see all the new frames. Where did you put my brass frames?'

'Keep looking. Come over this way,' I say,

335

leading her toward the dish cabinet. 'Would you like me to *set the table*?'

'Is it dinnertime?' asks Georgia, reliably literal.

'Where did you get these?' my mom asks, in a neutral tone.

'Don't you worry about that.'

'When did you do this?'

'Oh, you haven't seen the half of it. Need a spoon? A pot? A dish towel? A splash of hand soap?'

My mom's eyes dart around.

'Where is that picture of Booker?' she asks, looking at the windowsill over the sink.

'The fuzzy dark one?'

'I love that picture.'

'But look how cute this one is,' I say, handing her a black-and-white of Claire in the bath. 'And don't the frames look so nice together?'

'Oh, Kelly, she's naked,' she says, frowning. She once took a marker and scribbled a little black square on a picture of Georgia that showed the tippy-top of her tiny vagina. 'I assume you didn't throw anything out. You didn't, did you?'

'No, it's all in bags in the dining room.'

'Bags?' she asks, emphasizing the s.

'Well, at least come upstairs,' I say, wilting. 'Let me sit down for a minute, and have a glass of wine.' She's done. 'How long has your father been asleep?'

★ ★ ★

Eventually, after she sees the whole of it, she snaps.

'Kelly, I like my shower curtain.'

'It has a huge stain on the bottom.'

'I can wash it. I like my silverware. I don't need a new set of dishes. You know, it's just your father and me here. We don't need eight plates.' Her face is pinchy. 'How would you feel if I came to your house and started moving things around and changing everything?'

But I'm mad too. I want her to take better care of things, have higher standards, not be so old.

I remember when my mom's mom, Libby, stopped brushing her hair, when all she wore was one dress, with nylons and tan sneakers, every day.

'Mom, didn't you used to drive all the way to Baltimore to take Libby to get her hair done? Didn't you replace her old housedress that she loved with a blue one that she always said was scratchy? You did, Mom, I remember.'

I don't know why I do this. It's about as

futile as trying to smooth out a letter that's been folded; the creases will never go away.

'I hope you kept all the receipts,' she says.

Our coming fight is derailed by a phone call from Booker. His friend's dad has died of throat cancer and the funeral is tomorrow. Booker wants us to go, since he can't. My dad and I love the Roach family, so of course we'll go. Edward has a meeting, so my mom offers to take care of the girls. That'll give her time, I expect, to get every frame, dish, and towel back in the giant Bed, Bath & Beyond bags.

* * *

At the service, I am anxious and clingy, but Greenie is relaxed, at home even, making space in our pew for three guys my age whose dads died years back. He sings every hymn like it's an old favorite. Amen! Alleluia! He nods as the priest goes on about 'this life' and 'that life.' He seems so comfortable with mortality, totally engaged in life but somehow unattached to it, more Buddhist than I've ever been. I hold Greenie's hand throughout the eulogy. I run through all the times that knobby hand has been in mine — watching the flying monkeys in *The Wizard of Oz* or at early spring lacrosse games, the ones where it drizzles and blows but we stay anyway, or the night before my first chemo, or on a hundred walks down Wooded Lane 'just to show 'em we aren't a bunch of hothouse flowers.' I remember looking at Cleta's hands in her open casket and noticing with a wave of nausea how her veins were deflated. My dad's are plump like an old sailor's.

My stomach tightens and my face is flushed. I feel my head tighten and my vision blur and I know what's coming. I haven't had a panic attack in years, not since I was trying to make Stratford Studios work. I remember Priscilla, my therapist, and how she told me I have a great imagination that can take a tiny seed and grow a tall, thick hedge that blocks the view in every direction.

'Something that was just a thought,' Priscilla said, 'actually grows into a physical state, causing physical changes, like increased heart rate and rapid breathing.' The way she described my anxiety made me feel odd and special. She said I could learn to manage the attacks. 'When fear triggers your imagination and your imagination takes over, try to see it through. Keep making the movie, keep writing the scenes, until you see yourself surviving. Stay in the dream, let your body fly over the cliff, and then find a way to save yourself. Give that salvation as much color and detail as you give the fear. You need to convince yourself that it is possible to survive, that you, Kelly Corrigan, can survive.'

So as anxiety explodes inside me and the sounds of Mr. Roach's funeral fade, I follow Priscilla's directions. I keep making the movie.

I go to my dad's funeral.

I put on a black skirt and a gray top. I put my wet hair in a ponytail because I can't lift my arms to dry it. I slide into the backseat of a Town Car with my brothers and my mom and we hold hands and lean into one another and nobody says much of anything as we ride down Wooded Lane. Edward follows behind with the girls, who are godsends with their inappropriate juice boxes and Shamu dolls. The church is crammed like the pope was in town. We walk to the very first pew, past five rows of Corrigans, my uncles smiling at us, my Aunt Peggy crying because Greenie was hers too. Little Aunt Mary thinks about what to say to us after the service. My cousin Kathy smiles, knowing that it will get worse and better every day. The Lichtys are there from Little Rock, and Tracy Tuttle and Missy Carr came up together from DC. They understand.

One at a time, the priest welcomes us to the altar. Booker reads a poem and then slides back into the pew where Jen holds his arm. GT tells some great old stories and keeps clearing his throat, like that'll hold it all in. I go last. 'I am the lucky girl who gets to say, 'I was George Corrigan's daughter,'' and the rest is good and the words do as much as words can do, and then it's over and my uncles have to leave and I just can't let them go. I can't stop looking at their hair and their eyes and listening to the Baltimore in their voices, just like Greenie. I want Uncle Gene to tell me when I'll see him again. I want Jimmy and Dickie to promise to come to California.

I get to the part where the week is over and we pack up the girls and get on the plane.

I keep going, like Priscilla told me to. I unpack our bags in the home I've made for us. I do the laundry, line up a playdate, return a call about the new dishwasher I ordered. I change the sheets on the guest bed. I imagine my head on a wet pillow, staring across at Edward, who has no words left for these latest tears. Eventually, I hear Claire call out in the morning. I put a waffle in the toaster, I wash strawberries, I suck a drop of syrup off Georgia's fingertip.

I keep going, with those eyes looking up at me like I know what to do and I can make everything better.

And just like every other person who has buried his childhood, I grow up.

★ ★ ★

It's time to stand and repeat after the Father, 'Peace be with you.' Greenie puts his arm around me while we sing the processional. We file out. We linger in front of the church, seeing friends, hugging, saying what a nice service it was. We could do our father-daughter routine forever, but Edward and I are going back to California tomorrow. There's packing to do and girls to take care of. I tap Greenie's back and glance at my watch, shifting my weight forward. He nods. 'Yep, I better get you back to those girls.'

Epilogue

On August 4, 2005, after seven months of radiation and chemotherapy, my dad's bladder showed no discernable signs of cancer. I can't explain it and I won't ruin it by trying. My mother attributed it to all the prayers, hers chief among them, and called it 'a miracle,' making it clear for the first time that she had known all along a miracle was required. My dad's big line was, 'Tell 'em to take the Green Man off the endangered species list.'

A year later — a year in which my dad and I appeared on the *Today* show as a father-daughter survivor story and this book found a home at Voice — Greenie was back in touch with Dr. Schoenberg. More bloody urine.

My dad spent part of every day in treatment and the other part coaching as much lacrosse as he could handle and keeping tabs on the NCAA hoops tournament. I called Wooded Lane every day, usually while driving to Claire's preschool or watching Georgia cross the monkey bars. I called home to hear his exuberant voice say

'Lovey!' Because I could.

Finally, after sixty two-hour sessions in an oxygen tank (don't ask), Greenie's bladder stopped bleeding. His color returned. He stopped leaning on counters and passing on tennis games. My mom called me from the Jersey Shore to say that she was standing on the shoreline watching my dad bodysurf with some college lacrosse players he ran into.

This morning, after I hung up with Greenie, Georgia came in and worked her way into my lap. I asked her what makes a grown-up a grown-up, and she said, 'Growing.' Then I asked her what makes a home a home and she looked at me like I was playing a game unfairly and said, 'There's not a word for that.' And then, pushing off my desk to make the chair spin away from the bills, the phone, and the computer, she said, 'Can you just tell me a story?'

Someday, some later day, I'll find out what it is to be an adult — to bury someone essential, someone you don't think you can live without, someone attached in so many places you almost fall in after them.

'Please, Mommy — '

'Okay,' I say, giving her all of me, 'have I ever told you the story of the Green Flash?'

Acknowledgments

If you want to write a book, here's what I recommend:

Find yourself a Phoebe. She is the person who will read your first twenty pages and tell you you 'must' keep going. You will believe her because she is smarter than you and a better reader. She will share your draft with her old friend Jack, who used to work at ICM and has heard of a hot new agent there named Andrea Barzvi. She will look at your pages and start crying right there at her desk because she loved her dad and he had cancer too and he didn't make it.

Give your manuscript to Andy. She will share it with people like Bob Miller and Ellen Archer and Pamela Dorman and they will insist on making a proper book of it. They will make you feel so good when you meet them, like you have fallen into the nicest, brainiest book club. Ask to work directly with Kathleen Carr. You might not be able to get her; she'll be running the place soon. But oh, if you could get her! You will walk out of their offices beaming and then terrified that someone will discover that you are not a 'writer' so much as a housewife with a laptop.

Then, *and this is key*, at the next dinner party you go to, look for Kim Chisholm. She will become your new best friend and read every word of your manuscript many times. Not only will she teach you how to make an em dash in MS Word (it's harder than it looks) but she'll also help you make key lines a little funnier or a little more poignant.

After you have done all this, show the book to your parents. Your dad will say, 'Lovey, I'm blown away' as he pats his heart and your mom will make you cry by saying, 'Kelly, it's beautiful.' Your husband won't gush too much but you will overhear him talking about your writing in a way that gives you goose-bumps. Your children will not care a whit about any of it, until perhaps they are caught drinking at a dance and then they will pull your book off a shelf and ask you to read the prologue aloud.

We do hope that you have enjoyed reading this large print book.

Did you know that all of our titles are available for purchase?

We publish a wide range of high quality large print books including:
Romances, Mysteries, Classics
General Fiction
Non Fiction and Westerns

Special interest titles available in large print are:
The Little Oxford Dictionary
Music Book
Song Book
Hymn Book
Service Book

Also available from us courtesy of Oxford University Press:
Young Readers' Dictionary
(large print edition)
Young Readers' Thesaurus
(large print edition)

For further information or a free brochure, please contact us at:
Ulverscroft Large Print Books Ltd.,
The Green, Bradgate Road, Anstey,
Leicester, LE7 7FU, England.
Tel: (00 44) 0116 236 4325
Fax: (00 44) 0116 234 0205

Other titles published by
The House of Ulverscroft:

FOR THE LOVE OF JULIE

Ann Ming

When her twenty-two-year-old daughter Julie went missing in the night, Ann Ming was certain she had been murdered. Liaising with the police and looking after Julie's beloved three-year-old son, Ann waited desperately for news. Three months later she made a discovery that would devastate any mother. A violent local man, Billy Dunlop, had been tried for Julie's murder, but a series of blunders allowed him to walk free. Knowing he could not be tried again under the law of 'double jeopardy', he callously bragged about his 'perfect crime'. But Dunlop had not reckoned on Ann Ming . . .

DIRECT RED

Gabriel Weston

How does it feel to hold someone's life in your hands? What is it like to cut into someone else's body? What is it like to stand by, powerless, while someone dies because of the incompetence of your seniors? In this startlingly honest book, female surgeon Gabriel Weston answers the questions we have all wanted to ask about surgery. *Direct Red* tells the truth about what it is like to be a woman competing, in a world dominated by Alpha males, in the big-city hospitals of the twenty-first century.

BESPOKE

Richard Anderson

Richard Anderson quit school to become an apprentice on Savile Row and wound up owning his own shop on the world famous 'Golden Mile'. His clientele includes royalty, politicians and media stars. In February 1982, he started work at Savile Row's Henry Huntsman & Sons, earning just £2,000 a year, but his life changed forever. Richard's apprenticeship, overseen by the debonair Colin Hammick; grumpy eccentric Brian Hall; and the heroically overworked 'leg man' Dick Lakey, was seventeen years of rigorous practice in perfectionism. 'Young Richard' became, at thirty-four, the youngest head cutter in Huntsman's one hundred and fifty year history.